CRIMES OF THE BEATS

CRIMES OF THE BEATS

THE UNBEARABLES

AUTONOMEDIA

ISBN: 1-57027-069-4

Acknowledgements
The following pieces have previously appeared in other publications:
Denise Duhamel's "Beatnik Barbie" was published in her book *Kinky*
(Orchisis Press, 1997); Rob Hardin's "Di Prima: Ms. Fifty-Five" was published
in his short story collection *Distorture* (FC2/Black Ice Books, 1997); Ron
Kolm's "Man in the Grey Flannel Beret" first appeared in *Rant* #2; Tsaurah
Litzky's "Reflections on Beat Sexism" ran as one of her columns in *Downtown;*
Lance Olsen's "Cybermorphic Beat-Up Get-Down Subterranean Homesick
Reality-Sandwich Blues" was published in *Spitting Image* #2; Jerome Sala's
"Beatnik Stanzas" appeared in *Forehead* #2; Ron Sukenick's "The Fifteen
Minutes" was published in a slightly different version in the *American Book Review;*
David L. Ulin's "Beating a Dead Horse" originally appeared in the *San Francisco
Review of Books* under the title "And the Beats Go On"; Bob Witz' "Allen Ginsberg:
From Beatnik to Landmark" was published in *Rant* #2.
Mike Golden's "The Unbearable Beatniks of Light get Real!" and Lynne Tillman's
"Beats on the Beach" were published in the first Unbearables anthology, entitled
appropriately enough *Unbearables* (available from Autonomedia in paper at $12
plus $3 postage). We've included them because they *pertain.* (We're reprinting the
original version of Mike's story which appeared in *RedTape* #7 with the accompanying Art Spiegelman graphic.) We'd like to thank Jim & Ben & Isabel & Jordan &
Peter and all the rest of the Autonomedia collective for their encouragement and
production assistance, Ron Kolm for collecting the material, Jim Feast (who had the
original idea) for inputting the text, Susan Scutti for proofing it and Alfred Vitale for
his textual conceptualizations. We also wish to express our continuing gratitude to
Tuli Kupferberg and Rollo Whitehead,
without whom...

Autonomedia
POB 568 Williamsburgh Station
Brooklyn, New York 11211-0568

Phone & Fax: 718-963-2603
www.autonomedia.org

CONTENTS

GRAPHICS CREDITS

MIKE TOPP

LIFE

I was just, you know, I wasn't bothering anyone.

Jim Feast

Introduction to the Third 'Crimes of the Beats' Reading at the Cedar Tavern, November 12, 1995

O n November 12, 1945, shortly after the end of World War II, a wiry, troubled, trembling young poet stepped up to the improvised podium at a small San Francisco art gallery and began to speak:

"I have seen the—"

The showcase had been set up by a group of anarchist artists: principally Kenneth Rexroth, Gary Snyder and Hakim Bey, who had been interred as pacifists in a CO camp in Northern California, where they had become friends while translating Heidegger's *Sein und Zeit*.

It was their intention that this reading (partially captured on the legendary, now-lost film *Cool My Daisy*) would act to release some of the emotions that had been bottled up by the war. They picked the Big Sixpack Gallery as the best venue and the young prodigy Rollo Whitehead as the writer most likely to achieve this goal. He climbed onto the soapbox and began to recite in a robust tone that immediately brought a hush in the hall of rowdy expressionists. Many of those who stood stock-still had come to jeer but left worshipping.

"I have seen—"

To understand the genesis of this poem (and Rollo's friendship with Hakim), it is necessary to know more about prison conditions during the war. As the conflict burgeoned, the U.S. government engaged in massive repression of minorities and labor activists, jailing thousands of non-cooperators and non-conformists. The situation was so intense in California that a regulation was passed, little remembered now, that attempted to "decompress" the whole correctional world by doubling and tripling the prisoners in cells while folding together indiscriminately every branch of the state's vast penal apparatus.

So, by administrative fiat, cell 180J at San Quentin, in November 1944, contained the following: 1) Yoko Snapple (under the Japanese Retention Act), 2) Hakim Bey (CO, moved down from Quincy), 3) Man Mountain McBrain (Afro-American IWW organizer, suspected of industrial sabotage), 4) Carmellina Nosotros (Chicana, suspected smuggler), 5) Tess Ventricle (free love advocate, suspected prostitute) and 6) Rollo Whitehead (juvenile, suspected car thief).

It was during the all-night jabber sessions in this cell, which legend now calls "the little sixpack," that Whitehead enunciated his vocation as poet.

"I have—"

It could be said that at the date of the reading this beardless youth had yet to publish a poem, but this would be misleading, in that he refused later to publish anything, saying it would sully the purity of his spoken thought. Everything he wrote would be kept in his noggin and, if he forgot a line or a stanza, then, as he remarked, "It couldn't have been that memorable." However, his aversion to publication went beyond such a nice discrimination. To Rollo, ink had the quality of seepage. Bonding it, via the printing process, to a thought that previously had only air for a sounding board, made the ink melt like gooey chocolate, turning what had inchoately arisen all gummy and sooty. Even print as it appeared on a vid screen, Rollo was later to remark, was still shakily dead, contaminated by the charcoal embrace of pixillated light.

The real word, the dialogic word, *the legitimate word* was aerially borne, between two mouths, whether lipsticked or not, like those created during the muffled disputations under the blankets in cell 180J, carried on by match light, as evanescent as the tip of foam remaining from a just quenched beer.

Nonetheless, though this poem has never been published, I think the audience will recognize, if not the exact words of the piece, at least its contours, since this poem, circulating for years in an unauthorized bootleg version, was plundered by every "genius" in postmodern American literature.

Kenny introduced him. "I give you Rollo Whitehead."

The stripling, setting down his beer, began:

"I have seen the *worst* minds of my generation destroyed by madness,

starving, hysterical, clothed,

dragging themselves through the caucasian streets at noon,

looking for a bar of soap..."

I'll stop there so we can get on with the real business of the night, a genealogical presentation of how the Unbearables got their inspiration and lost their name through an acquaintance with the works of Rollo and his school.

What? Is old Jim slipping?

No, you heard right. Rollo didn't help us acquire but lose our collective moniker.

Here's the story. You know how, when you first meet someone, you're inclined to give them their full title. Mr. Ronald Aloysius Kolm, for example. But, as time runs on, some of the proprieties drop away. A charming informality slips in. You go from Mr. Ronald Kolm to Ronald Kolm to Ron Kolm to Ron K., Ron and, finally, you're down to Rrrr.

You may have heard that the Unbearables originally took the name—supplied by Mike Golden—of the Unbearable Beatniks of Life, and may have supposed that the name gradually got shorter through the same sort of process by which a friend's name over the years is reduced to usable proportions. Not so. This was all conscious choice; strategy, you might say. After going with our original title for a few years, through much of the '70s, we discovered that most of us hate life. So, we eliminated one word and became known as the Unbearable Beatniks of. A couple of more years passed and one of our more circumspect members—Sharon Mesmer—pointed out that a preposition without an object was ungrammatical. We became the Unbearable Beatniks. However, after our research for this reading, when we became privy to the vile treatment accorded Rollo, Yoko, Man Mountain and other true originals by the leaders of this sect and, further, found how Rollo's poems and even his thoughts had been misappropriated by this cult, we lopped off the noun Beatniks. From tonight, November 12, 1995, we will be known as Unbearables.

Beyond the misappropriation and sentimentality, the Beat Generation had one overriding flaw. Not in literary skill, ability to probe society's sore spots, lifestyle, wit, pathos, prosody or such areas. Our group is unconcerned with such matters anyway. Our primary interest is in how writers are grouped. This is where the Beats had their down-fall.

Let's do a comparison. Think of the writers of the thirties and the fifties. They were pretty similar in theme. *The Grapes of Wrath, On the Road,* everybody's driving up and down the highways, for various reasons. In both periods, every American novel has its obligatory trip to Mexico, in *The 42nd Parallel* as much as in *The Soft Machine.* With all these similarities, why are the writers of the thirties so much better than the later ones?

If we compare organizational charts from the two periods, we can see where the problems arise.

The first chart shows the hierarchy of the Beats. You will note that is it pyramidal in form, with Ginsberg at the apogee and Ferlinghetti and Snyder right below. You'll see, too, that all the female and minority writers—Brenda Frazer, Leroi Jones, etc., are firmly at the bottom. That goes for those from the proletariat as well—the example of Neal

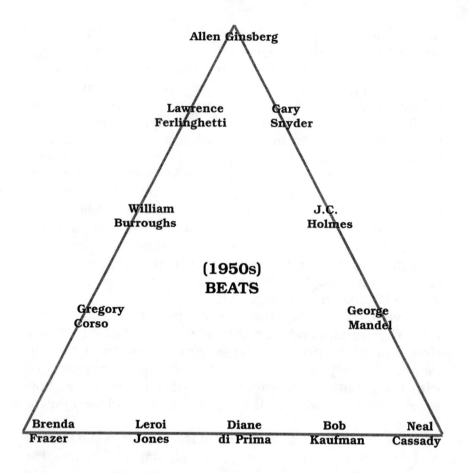

Allen Ginsberg

Lawrence Ferlinghetti   Gary Snyder

William Burroughs   J.C. Holmes

(1950s)
BEATS

Gregory Corso   George Mandel

Brenda Frazer   Leroi Jones   Diane di Prima   Bob Kaufman   Neal Cassady

Cassady makes this clear. Now if Bob Kaufman, for instance, wanted to get a poem published, he would first have to get it approved by Bill Burroughs, who would then, in turn, have to obtain the approval of Ferlinghetti, who, finally, would have to pass it up to Ginsberg for the last stamp.

Next let's look at the second chart, which reveals the system obtaining in the thirties. The superiority of the arrangement is immediately evident. Sure, there is a rigid pyramidal structure, as before, but there are two pyramids.

The first, composed of the publishing empire of the Communist Party, is ruled over by Granville Hicks. Seconds-in-command are John Steinbeck and Henry Roth.

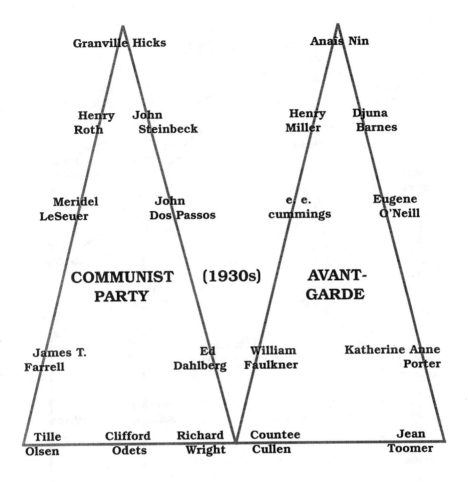

COMMUNIST PARTY (1930s) **AVANT-GARDE**

Granville Hicks

Henry Roth — John Steinbeck

Meridel LeSeuer — John Dos Passos

James T. Farrell — Ed Dahlberg

Tille Olsen — Clifford Odets — Richard Wright

Anais Nin

Henry Miller — Djuna Barnes

e.e. cummings — Eugene O'Neill

William Faulkner — Katherine Anne Porter

Countee Cullen — Jean Toomer

But see, there is also a second structure, the power pyramid of the avant garde, topped by Anais Nin and with Henry Miller and Djuna Barnes on the second tier.

The greater opportunities offered to minorities, women and proletarians in this time are undeniable, although the discerning among you will have noted that the base of the structures are still reserved for the disadvantaged. What is particularly appealing about this organization is the greater artistic freedom prevailing. If Tillie Olsen, for example, as a Communist, submitted a novel to Steinbeck and it was rejected, she still had the option of slightly altering the ending and submitting it to e.e. cummings, hoping to find approval in the second hierarchy.

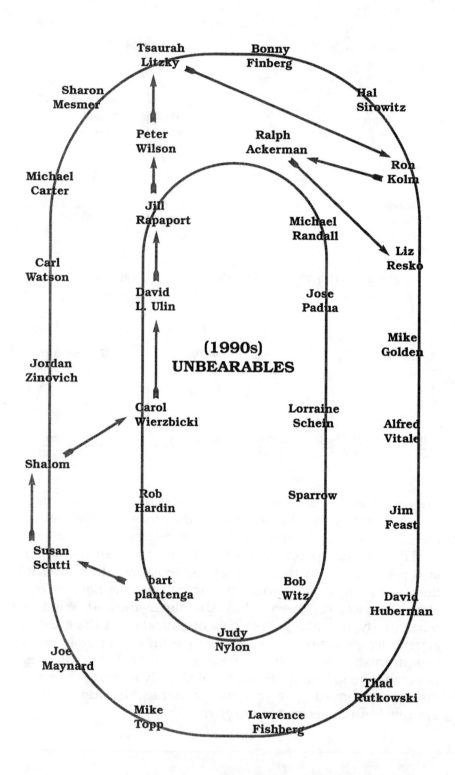

Finally, let us take a peek at the most progressive organizational form of the nineties, that of the Unbearables. You'll see that it consists of two ellipses one inside the other. Scientists call these shapes "vulvic curves." They should not be imagined as standing up, but laying flat on a table or bed so that there is no uppermost or lowermost portion.

The discerning in the audience may have already noted a potential difficulty with transmission along this grid. Suppose bart plantenga wanted to make a submission to Liz Resko's magazine. He would have to give his piece to Susan Scutti, who would forward it to Shalom who would pass it to Carol Wierzbicki who would mail it to David Ulin who would hand it to Jill Rapaport who would transfer it to Peter Wilson who would pass it along it to Tsaurah Litzky who would see that it got to Ron Kolm who would transport it to Ralph Ackerman who would, when he ran into her, give it, rather crumpled by now, to Liz. This would seem to make for some insupportable bottlenecks. However, I have been keeping back one key bit of information. Both ellipses are constantly turning. So, rather than sending his short story on a contorted journey, if bart wanted Liz's editorial attention, he would merely sit back and wait till she rotated by.

I think you will all attest to how much better our structure is than the former ones and, as to how much better our writing is, due to this organization, you can judge as the night proceeds.

It's time to begin, but, perhaps, before starting, you would like to echo in your hearts, the prayer I am about to offer.

"Thank god, I have nothing. Help me not to hate those that I must destroy."

Lynne Tillman

Beats on the Beach

There was shit everywhere, garbage and fat bodies and rotting hot dogs and I was disgusted on the beach. The scene was coming down around me and I stared at the ocean, melancholy and lonely, green and cool, and far away, way out there, was Europe and history and the ghosts of Baudelaire and Rimbaud and those very alive French girls —the green waves were their breasts rising and falling something like my cock when I'm horny, needy and angry as a dirty syringe, on those rocky nights of the soul. But not now, not today.

O inconstancy—I had to concentrate because of the shit on the beach, those straight surfer goons strutting around and kicking sand, and me, haggard, stretched tight like a drum over this mad existence, burned out, my whole body a night yellow white except for my left hand, the one I hang out the driver's window to feel the cool American breeze rush crazily over my American skin. Sometimes when I'm rolling along the highway of dreams, I let that hand lay on top of the roof of the car like I don't have a care in the world and my dog's next to me, grinning like an idiot, happy the way a dog can be, his short hindlegs on the backseat, his head resting next to my shoulder, content as I drive along. My dog, the one I left with Riva, Riva the dancer, she just kissed me goodbye and whispered—Later, baby.

I shot a glance at Allen who was smiling in his strange inward cerebral way because he was thinking of something bigger that wasn't on the beach

—What a chick Riva was, man. She'd make your hair curl, if you had any.

The Beanbag—that's what we called him—turned to me and muttered, Leave it alone, Fast Jack, suck on your own dick for a while. Don't get angry, my man, I answered, and I swore I would love him until the day I die which might be tomorrow because tomorrow always comes and how many tomorrows does any man have.

I dug him, I did. Allen was America's bearded idealist, hopeful and scared but eager and ready to face Life when it happened, a true poet, the kind I was striving to be, because I wanted to live the Life with everything in me, to be Real in the face of phony gutless pathetic humanity, the human subspecies, but here on the beach Allen looked weird, a skinny New York intellectual on the sand near the ocean, all pale and frail and gray around the edges from long nights in clubs talking the smart hip talk to other hipsters of the future, and sometimes I thought about him, us, because if you split us open, you'd find bars, bottles, tables and chairs, but in him, there would be books and bookcases, addresses, a card catalogue and eyeglasses, BECAUSE he—we're the poets of airless, smoky rooms, word makers in the hidden factories of the American spirit.

Life is shit and you have to be ready to give it up, ride off on an endless road to nowhere, disappear in a hotel room so ugly even Wild Bill would snicker at the cliché, his eyes half-closed while he's nodding, high on some heavy shit that gives him the vision he needs to see right through the merciless nothing of everything. Allen wanted me, I didn't want him, I wanted someone, Wild Bill hungered for Allen, they were making the scene.

—Hey, Beanbag, rub a little of that on my back.

Allen looked up kind of stunned like he was just born and I had to laugh at his beautiful ignorance and his innocence. He didn't even know he was on the beach, his head in a book while I was watching some cute little girls walking by and thinking how it was in high school and how my mom loved me, but I don't want to think about that, about the past, how I only had orgasms when I fantasized about her leaving me, and it's sad for eternity. Allen rubbed some lotion on my white back which was turning color under the wild rays of the heartless sun. The imperturbable ocean rolling and roiling let me forget for a minute the people somewhere else toiling and sweating, working their insides out—for what, for a buck, for what else in this stinking world, and those politicians with their platitudinous cant, it makes me sick, even on the beach, because which way to turn, to look. I gotta look so I do.

Out of nowhere the Marvelous Magi from Hell comes toward us, Wild Bill wearing a djellabah that covers him like a tent so no one can see the frozen rivers that are his veins and the scabrous body he calls home. I've seen that expression on Wild Bill's face before, when he's thinking of what he's lost or the midwest or history, a so-what, a Is This All There Is? Wild Bill lights a cigarette with a match that appears like he did out of nowhere—the ether—and he sits down on the blanket next to The Beanbag, who's dousing his own white hairy body with suntan lotion.

Wild Bill snorts—That crummy lotion your cover story, Allen, you think the agents of the Polyester Poison Sunboy won't find you here? Won't get you? Ah, relax, Beanbag, the Black Meat Mamas don't want your skinny ass. I've got something in my pocket that'll melt you into just so many lumps of carcinogenic plasm.

The Beanbag and Wild Bill kissed a long time and I lost myself in them, their sticky bodies, their wet mouths merged into one enormous American soul kiss, it was gorgeous. Boom. And I remembered that little blond girl in Cincinnati and how I loved her but couldn't stay, because I never can, can't stay in love with one, because I'm in love with the One and All, but then I thought about poetry and prose, how the word could illuminate if I could just find it, the right word. Like Wild Bill who can—he writes and there's blood on the page, he spills his guts and I don't mean metaphorically, I'm talking about real blood on the page, so thick and dark that Allen can't read the words underneath without scraping it off and dumping it on the floor.

The sun was beating down and later Allen was goofing to Wild Bill about another poet, Bra Man—this cat, The Beanbag was wailing now, thinks pantie raids are bourgeois, that's why he steals chicks' boobie traps—that's what he calls them—and we laughed a long time, but really Allen wanted to be in Paris or Tangier, away from the indifferent ugliness of America, but when I leave I feel homesick, homesick in my depths, and I just don't know.

I get so lonely, even here on the beach, and Wild Bill says, Fast Jack, grab yourself a beer and watch some TV, the way you always do and have, and always will, and Bill is right, that's what I do, that's what I did, I can't change, I am what I am, a man. And that's all there is, that and the beach, the bigger than life ocean and the grains of sand, they're like miracles, wonders in this Mongolia of existence. It gets me, really, this beauty, and it keeps me hooked to Life.

But watching Wild Bill and The Beanbag I knew I was really alone, with them but not with them, I never did dig men, not that way, because that's not my scene, so I was with them and not with them, and they understood, and it was cool, and I would move on, leave, the way I always leave, I have to leave everybody.

I popped open another beer and patted my stomach which was getting bigger every day. Allen says I look like I'm carrying his baby and, you know, I'd dig that, to give birth to his baby, to put something in the world, not just words— well, words too because they're important, poetry is the Truth—but a baby who'd grow up and drive across the country, his hand lying on the roof of the car, the American breeze blowing, my boy who'd say one day—fast Jack was my dad and he was cool.

MICHAEL RANDALL

KEROUAC HAIKU

blind drunk at mom's house
middle of the afternoon:
On the Road Part Two

ON THE ROAD HAIKU

where were they going?
my guess: somewhere to escape
Ginsberg's hairy ass

A little less than a year before his death, Jack Kerouac (center above, and below) appeared on William F. Buckley's television program "Firing Line". During the program, he confessed to Republican party-line conservatism and assailed the protest movement "Hippies" of the 1960's, (here represented by writer Ed Sanders, above right).

B. Kold

Jack and Barbie

Americans generally regard writers as morally-sus-
pect losers, enemies not only of the state but all that
is good and clean and pure. Introduce yourself at a
party as a writer and people react as if you confessed to ped-
dling child pornography—which, in a sense, any good writer
does. Only recently did I begin to understand how this disdain is instilled during childhood. If you're about my age—
thirtysomething—you'll no doubt remember the board game
"Mystery Date." Back in my day, board games were generally male territory—boys played "Monopoly" for financial
training, or "Risk" to learn warmongering—girls got Barbie
dolls and Suzy Homemaker and so on. The "Mystery Date"
game was the exception to this rule. Me, I never played
"Mystery Date," due to my involuntary gender, but I saw
enough TV commercials for it to understand its object: dating Mr. Right. Come game's end, you got to open the front
door of the colonial house and meet your blind date; win-
ners got "The Dream," a blond, crew-cut, broad-shouldered
boy wearing a letter sweater. Losers drew "The Dud," a
slack-looking fellow with shaggy black hair, jeans and a
flannel shirt, windbreaker jacket carelessly slung over his
slooping shoulder. Now, I hadn't seen a "Mystery Date" commercial in twenty-odd years or so until it was recently featured on some TV news item about folks who collect not only
antique toys (when the junk from your childhood is considered antique, you know you ain't getting any younger), but
their accompanying publicity as well. They ran the crucial

23

footage from the "Mystery Date" commercial: "Will he be a dream—or a dud?" and when "The Dud" door opened, revealing the kind of guy these little girls were being taught to avoid like the plague, I finally comprehended something I never wished to know about these United States as I recognized his vaguely handsome, unshaven, sardonic face— "The Dud" was none other than Jack Kerouac.

Thaddeus Rutkowski

Jack Kerouac's Infraction

As a player on the Columbia University football team, Jack Kerouac practices blocking by side-stepping at the line of scrimmage and bringing his fist down on the back of his opponent's skull. The move usually leads to the charging player eating dirt. Off the field, Kerouac often hangs out with his teammates in Greenwich Village. There, in the land of tambourines, the following unfortunate incident occurs: The Columbia players come across a man with a violin. They chase him into an alley, grab the violin and smash it over his head.

Later, on the road, Kerouac remembers the shameful act of ka-bonging. In the cursed city of Pittsburgh, he sees the violinist's rabbit-eyed face. Amid the bop and jazz of Chi-town, he hears the twang of snapping catgut. In the wild humming night of L.A.'s Central Avenue, he feels the instrument splinter in his hands. Back in the absolute madness of New York, he walks through his guilt over beaning the sissy.

Later still, at the end of the Sixties, he remembers the violin-smashing with pride. He contrasts his decisiveness to the clownish behavior of his spiritual progeny, people who should have memorized the Beat Generation's teaching, people like Abbie Hoffman and Jerry Rubin, Peter Fonda and Dennis Hopper, Papa John Phillips and Country Joe McDonald. But, as it turns out, he cannot abide their agit-prop antics. He would much rather stride the streets with purpose, maybe kick some milquetoast butt with William F. Buckley Jr., than mingle with the flower hairs.

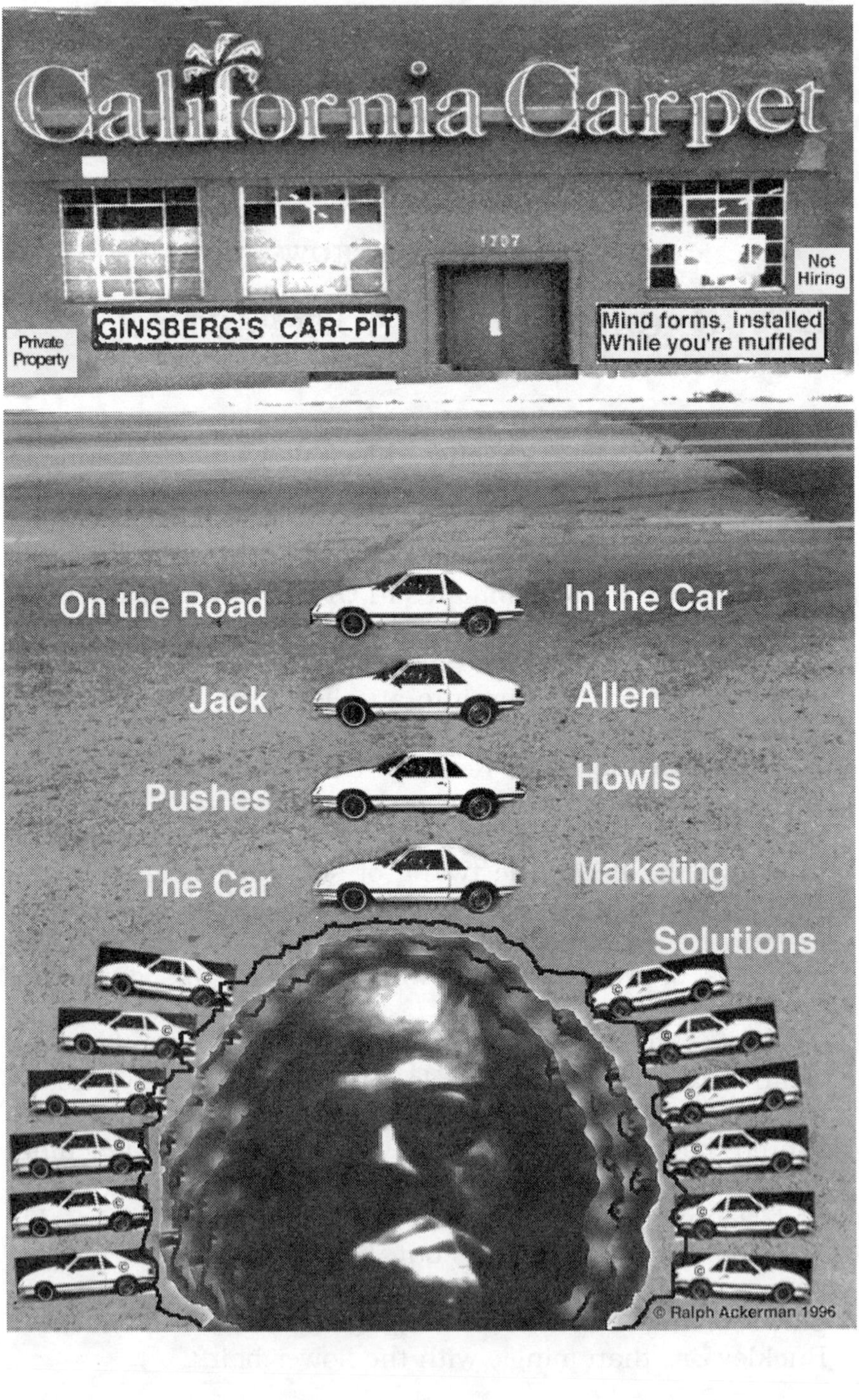
California Carpet
Not Hiring
GINSBERG'S CAR-PIT
Private Property
Mind forms, installed
While you're muffled
On the Road
In the Car
Jack
Allen
Pushes
Howls
The Car
Marketing
Solutions
© Ralph Ackerman 1996

JIM FEAST

BEAT PLAYLET

*E*nter Jack Kerouac to Yoko Snapple and Rollo Whitehead

Jack

Boy, am I great. Yoko, doll baby. I dropped by your crib — Hey, what do we have here? Rollo. Jingling huckleberries, I haven't seen you in a stone's age. You still drinking lead balloons down at Sudsy's, you loser? Ha. Ha.

Rollo

Shut the fuck up.

Rollo turns and sits facing away from the audience.

Jack

You jealous son of a bitch. My new book came out, *Mexico City Blues*, and he's green with envy. I'm really getting famous and the more famous I get, the greater I get.

You see, being famous made me a better person. I realized people didn't just love me for my talent, but for who I am.

Yoko

And who are you, Jack?

Jack

The greatest minister of a new-fangled, popped-up, propped-up version of a desexed Mahayana Buddhism as well as the greatest non-playing bebop musician on earth.

Yoko

Is that what your book's about?

Jack

No. Boy, am I great. It's the tale of how I suffered like a saint to rescue our great country from ruin.

Yoko

And how have you accomplished that?

Jack

I'm trying to get our people to give up on moribund, self-serving, old hat Christianity so they can adopt a silly Oriental religion.

Yoko

Thanks for saying shit.

Jack

But—

Yoko

Shut the fuck up. Japanese women are sick to death with the ball-less posturing of you Yankee imperialist hep-cats. I say "ball-less" because you don't have the guts to admit that you benefit from exploiting us. You go to Mexico, use the whorehouse, get a good exchange rate; then pretend you're not a tourist. And why? What is this distinction between you and the average ugly American? You say a tourist is a poseur and you are only wearing a mask.

But what mask, daddio? The mask of Buddha. Japan girls are sick of this rotten Buddha. I mean, it's bad enough when your boss tells you life is a meaningless veil of Maya so you shouldn't complain as he cheats and squeezes you. We know where that comes from. But to hear an uncircumcised, drunk out of his mind stumblebum demanding rich man's privilege—the privilege of preaching phony baloney spirituality to the poor—that's too much.

You ruined my Rollo, but you won't get me.

Jack

I never touched Rollo's ass.

Yoko

He drank too deep at your well, frat boy. Too deep.

Rollo turns around with a needle sticking in his arm

Rollo

The world has changed, Jackie. All changed. Because the streets have changed. You see, it's the streets that determine everything else. And the streets are more hardcore, man. So the world is more hardcore.

Rollo collapses.

Yoko

This is all your fault, you no count beatnik wastrel. Get out of here Kerouac, and never darken my pad again.

Jack (exits, muttering in a low voice)
Boy, am I great.

EVERT EDEN

CRIME #1001 OF THE BEATS: ARRANT DISILLUSIONMENT

When I was ten in South Africa, being raised as an elite fascist, I one day encountered an amazing article in the *Sunday Times* of South Africa.

It was on the back page, usually reserved for sensational reports about a preacher's daughter who became a stripper, or a rich man's wife found in bed with the gardener.

This Sunday there was a report about a group of writers in America — the beats or beatniks. They congregated in dark clubs, where they practiced such dire activities as jazz, drugs, reading poetry out loud, and free love.

That evening at dinner I announced my deepest ambition to my family.

"I want to be a beatnik," I said.

My folks were shocked. They knew it was terribly wrong, but did not know what to say.

One week later my mother came up with a reply. "You can't be a beatnik," she said. "You're too fond of taking a bath."

A few weeks ago I heard Jack Kerouac read one of his poems on NPR, from a collection of his spoken word pieces on CD.

So I wrote this short requiem:

Jack, oh! Jack!
your name rhymes with Kerouac
I thought you were so cool
but now I heard your poem
in which you say
how hip you are
cause you dig the patois
and jazz these black cats play

but you sound
Jack, oh! Jack!
like the worst whiteboy appropriation
Jack, oh! Jack!
though your name rhymes with Kerouac
I heard you in stereo
and you turned out just another hero
with feet of claymation
Jack, oh! Jack!
you were the Vanilla Ice
of your generation

GENERAL OPEN CALL

Jack Kerouac's

ON THE ROAD

CASTING

For the AMERICAN ZOETROPE film

CASTING for the roles of SAL PARADISE, DEAN MORIARTY, CARLO MARX, MARYLOU, CAMILLE, BULL LEE, ED and GALATEA DUNKEL, and all supporting roles.

Mr. Francis Ford Coppola will personally conduct the auditions.

Please bring an 8x10 photo or snapshot and an audio cassette (non-returnable 1 minute maximum) reading from ON THE ROAD, or other of your choice from MELVILLE, JACK LONDON, THOMAS WOLFE, RIMBAUD, YEATS, MARK TWAIN, WALT WHITMAN, PROUST, SPENGLER, DOS PASSOS, WILLIAM CARLOS WILLIAMS, WILLIAM BURROUGHS, KEROUAC (VISIONS OF CODY), or GINSBERG (HOWL).

Simple dress and hair from the period (1947-1952) encouraged. Both SAG and Non-Guild members will be seen.

AUDITIONS

TO BE HELD AT

SAINT PAUL THE APOSTLE AUDITORIUM

10 COLUMBUS AVENUE
(between 59th & 60th Street)
NEW YORK CITY

FEBRUARY 4TH
12 NOON TO 7PM ONLY

SHARON MESMER

ON THE 'ON THE ROAD' LINE

Peggy was in line with her friend Lois, an actress currently starring in a Rochester community theater production of "You're A Good Man Charlie Brown."

"I flew in yesterday from Arizona just to stand in line with her! Her mother was a hippie in the '60's and told her to audition. We don't even know what *On The Road* is!"

And it wasn't just a line — it was a good, old-fashioned *happening*: the open casting call for Francis Ford Coppola's movie version of *On The Road* drew, by rumored estimate, 5,000 wannabeats out of their cozy domiciles and into the slushy aftermath of the year's first snowstorm.

Beleaguered yet eager faces peered out of hoods, hats and snoods as I treaded over icy patches and hardened snowdrifts to find my place in a line that began at the door of St. Paul the Apostle auditorium on Ninth Avenue and culminated at the western end of 60th Street. A clutch of partying pot smokers welcomed me; icy white breaths rose continually like early morning steam from manhole covers; expertly pommaded hair and 1950's-style make-up jobs were ruined by wind and weather everywhere.

I arrived amid salutes and waves from my new line-mates.

"Hey! It's just like standing in line for concert tickets when you were a teenager, right?"

"Yeah, but I was a teenager then, so it seemed like fun."

Nods of approval all around. My mates for the duration were Daria, a Hawaiian-born actress who was hoping for the role of Terry, the Mexican girl; Arizona Peggy and Rochester Lois; a tall German model who spoke no English and her boyfriend, Wimpe ("Not Wim-pee — VIM-PAY! VIM-PAY!"), a performance artist from Berlin; and a quiet guy whose pommaded hair had yet to fall apart.

"Hey, are you a performance artist?" Arizona asked. "You look like a performance artist. Doesn't she?" Rochester nodded.

"Yeah," I said. "I just finished a gig with Spalding Gray at La Mama called 'Simone de Beauvoir Offered Me A Tampon.' I played Mick Jagger and Spalding Gray played Simone de Beauvoir."

Arizona and Rochester were dumbfounded. Daria snickered, lighting a Galoise: "Hey, who do you think they'll get to play Kerouac?"

Rochester was confused: "Who? Who's that?"

"I heard Keanu," Daria continued.

"I hear Christian *Slay-ta*," said Wimpe.

"Yeah," I said, "but that's only because River Phoenix is dead."

"RIVER PHOENIX IS DEAD?" Arizona and Rochester were shocked. They conferred a moment, then silently left the line. A red-headed guy carrying coffee bumped into them and slipped on the ice, but managed to keep the coffee from spilling. Rising, holding the cup aloft to cheers, he replaced the young mourners.

"Ya know," he said, excitedly, "there are all these rumors going around on the line! Like Coppola's not even looking at anyone over twenty-six!"

"Or redheads," said Daria.

"I hear he ist cazting das major roles, ja," Germany offered.

"I know for a fact that Ginsberg's in there with him!" I announced. The mention of Ginsberg touched off a wave of "brushes with greatness" tales farther up in the line, amongst the older hopefuls. One guy claimed he sat in the booth behind Ginsberg at Kiev Kitchen once; one girl said she almost enrolled in the "*Europa* Institute"; a couple argued over whether it was Ginsberg or e.e. cummings who wrote that poem about the red wheelbarrow. Just then a roar sounded from the corner of 60th and Ninth.

"Mein Gott, iz dat a riot?" Wimpe wondered.

"I think it's someone reciting 'Howl!'" Red quipped.

Daria shook her head: "Naw, it's probably those pot smokers turning the corner. That's the last milestone."

"Vas ist dis *milestone?*" Wimpe asked, alarmed.

"Well, the first milestone is the parking garage, then the next one is the laundry room air vent, then comes the chain link fence — you can actually see St. Paul's at that point — and then the corner up there. Whenever a group turns the corner they cheer."

Suddenly I caught sight of my friend David Huberman, international ranter, making his way to the end of the line.

"Hey, funny seeing you here!" I said.

"Whaddarya talkin' about? I been in fifteen plays this year!"

"Oooh, touchy..." Daria mumbled.

Red nodded righteously: "That's okay. The line'll take the fight outta him. It's the great equalizer!"

And as David stomped off it was time to play "Spot the Celebrities." Daria began:

"Okay, there's Natalie Merchant...and up there's Jeff Goldblum, hoping for the Ginsberg part...and there's Truman Capote, back from the dead to audition for the Herbert Huncke part...and here comes Famous Amos!"

A black guy with grey hair handed cookies out along the line: "You all gotta keep up your strength! I live in that apartment building right there, and I feel for you! Good luck! Good luck to you all!"

Soon we reached the first milestone, the parking garage. The line snaked in along the wall, curved to the right, then snaked out along the other wall. Daria and I were able to check out those who had arrived in line behind us.

"That guy's too fat...there aren't any fat people in *On The Road.*"

"Does that old lady think she's gonna play Kerouac's mom?"

Red jumped in: "And check out that black girl. There aren't any black girls in *On The Road!*"

"Yeah, what does she think this is," I said, "*The Subterraneans?*"

Red looked confused: "The Sub-*what??* What's that?"

Fat snowflakes had begun falling while we stood in the garage. I suddenly began to think about how cold it would get once it got dark. Then I remembered I'd had nothing to eat since eleven that morning.

"Ya know, I should eat this granola bar I packed."

"And you know what's gonna happen then, doncha?" Daria cautioned. "All the blood's gonna go to your stomach!"

"Maybe she should put the granola bar in her shoes!" Red added.

I was right: by the time we were out on the street again the sun had gone down and the wind had picked up. The entire line was hopping and stamping, and a breath-vapor fog formed above us like a cloud of unknowing. A tradition began, of spelling those who went across the street to warm up in the Roosevelt Hospital Emergency Room. Wimpe was opposed to this:

"Vy varm up? You vill jus' get *colt* again, ja?" His girl-friend's cheekbones were now creating a wind tunnel.

Daria laughed: "Yeah, and why bother getting sober when you're just gonna be drunk again? Why shower when you're just gonna stink again?"

A girl in black beret and miniskirt, legs bare, trudged past.

"Oh, right... she won't last five minutes," I said.

The cute quiet guy, his pommaded hair finally fallen, spoke up: "Yeah, I'm wearing thermal socks and boots and I think I've got hypothermia!"

Red perked up: "Hey, let's go to the Emergency Room! Then we'll spell these guys when we get back!"

"We'll never see them again," I predicted.

"Yeah. Soul-mates. See, that's the good thing about an ordeal like this: you never know who you're gonna meet!"

"I wish I'd meet a warm front from the Gulf of Mexico right now!"

"Listen, why don't you go to the Emergency Room for fifteen minutes, and then you can spell me when I go."

Agreed, and I was glad. But the scene in the ER wasn't much better than the one outside: security guards were chasing people out.

"But this is fucking hospital!" a feisty, raspberry beret-ed young lady announced. "You're supposed to take care of people here!" The beefy guard put his hand on his holster, ready for action.

"Well, do you wanna see a doctor?"

"Yeah, goddammit! I'll see a doctor! Get me a fuckin' doctor!"

Reinforcements were radioed in and soon we were back

on the street. I figured I'd go get some coffee. In The Flame restaurant I ran into David Huberman again.

"Ya know I saw Michael Carter when I first got here, and he said he got in through a secret door!"

"So why didn't you do that?"

"'Cause as he was tellin' me I was goin' over my lines for Susan Sherman's play in my head and I couldn't hear what he was sayin'. Are you goin' back in line?"

"Yeah, I just came in here to get coffee. Hey look! There's that security guard who kicked everybody out of the hospital!" I turned and shouted to the group who'd just been thrown out: "Hey! There's the creep that kicked us out of the hospital!" The guard became like Christ taunted by centurions: "Ya creep! Ya little dickwad! Hey! Asshole! Ya dropped yer scrotum!"

When the guard actually looked down to see where his scrotum lay a roar went up from the crowd.

"Our ordeal has not been in vain!" I announced. But I was wrong.

Back outside I discovered my group had finally gotten in — without me! An order had been issued from the inside to let bigger groups of people in now that it had gotten late, and I'd missed my chance! Missed my chance! I couldn't join the line, as the end was at the point where I'd started three hours ago. There was nothing to do. I blew it.

From a phone booth as half-broken as my spirits I called my boyfriend:

"I'm a loser! A miserable failure! I don't deserve to live!"

He suggested we meet for dinner at Two Boots on Avenue A.

"Oh, because that's the official restaurant of losers, failures, and never-wases?"

"No it's not! Remember we saw Roland Gift there?"

"Yeah, and after Fine Young Cannibals broke up look how his career took off!"

And sure enough, who should be sitting in the booth behind ours but the living symbol of my misery: Conan O'Brien, explaining "Exile On Main Street" to three giggling women.

"Things could be worse, ya know," my boyfriend said.

"Yeah," I moaned, my hands covering my face, "it could be Alan Thicke."

DAVID L. ULIN

BEATING A DEAD HORSE

O n October 21, 1989, a friend and I went to Lowell, Massachusetts to commemorate the twentieth anniversary of Jack Kerouac's death. I don't know what exactly we were hoping to find there — some sense of closure, perhaps, some idea that Kerouac and all the things he had written were actually real and not merely figures of our collective imaginations, some way to put him and his influence on our lives into perspective. I'd been engaged in this sort of process for years, re-reading Kerouac's books on occasional cross-country jaunts, trying to match literature with geography to give *his* words a place in *my* world, more than just descriptions of a bygone past but mirrors of my own experience, or, at least, the parts of it that could correspond to his.

Whatever it was we were looking for, though, Lowell that day was nothing like we had expected. There was no mention of Kerouac in the pages of *The Lowell Sun*, where he'd once worked briefly as a sportswriter, no indication of his presence at the homes he had lived in as a boy, nor in the church where his funeral had taken place. On the narrow red-brick downtown streets, residents were stupefied by our requests for directions to the Kerouac Memorial, dedicated with great fanfare only a year or two before. Even when, after better than an hour of futile meandering, we finally found it — an arrangement of marble slabs engraved with excerpts from his books, erected in a small park on the banks of the Merrimack River

— my friend and I were the only people around. In the city where he had grown up, a city which he had recreated so lovingly in so much of his writing, there seemed little room left to remember Jack Kerouac, almost as if he had never been.

Of course, it might be easier to get a grasp on Kerouac if that were true, if he *were* just a mythic invention, a manifestation of what he called the "generation of furtives" who came of age with the first Atomic bomb. Certainly, he was a product of that era, his theories of spontaneous prose as much a reaction to the fractured realities of the post-World War II world as were, say, Jackson Pollock's action paintings, or the blistering small combo bop sounds of Beat heroes Charlie Parker and Dizzy Gillespie. The temptation to view him in such simple terms is particularly seductive because — as with Pollock and Parker — Kerouac's premature death denied him the chance to grow creatively, to shed old ideas and shift directions, to continue to develop with the times. In fact, with so much of his work written in a massive creative surge between 1947 and 1957, he may have deprived himself of those opportunities even if he'd stayed alive. His later years, after all, were largely spent in dissolution and heavy drinking, and, by 1965, as astute a critic as Seymour Krim was already pointing out that "[t]he danger now confronting Kerouac, and it looms large, is one of repetition. He can add another dozen hardcover spurts to his 'Duluoz Legend'...but unless he deepens, enlarges or changes his pace they will only add medals to an accomplishment already achieved — they will not advance his talent vertically or scale the new meanings that a man of his capacity should take on."

Krim's comments are important because they focus on the idea of *intention*, the fundamental factor at the heart of Kerouac's — or any artist's — career. Sure, his books created a mythological vision of America at mid-century; sure, they encouraged countless impressionable readers — myself included — to take to the highways and see this country for the vast sprawl of possibility that it once was. But this doesn't mean they were in any way inevitable — that is, work which would have come along regardless of whether or not

Kerouac was around to create it. Instead, the endless tor-
rent of Kerouac's words was primarily the result of his own
need to re-invent *himself*, a need that had less to do with the
time in which he lived than it did with his demons and
obsessions, his conception of what was important, and of
how he saw his place within the world.

Unfortunately, however, when we think of Jack Kerouac
today, it's more the legend we remember than the intention,
more the image he has left us with than the work. Unlike his
aging buddies Allen Ginsberg, William S. Burroughs, and
Gary Snyder — just to name a few — Kerouac is frozen in
our imaginations as he was in the late 1950s, the thirty-five
year old King of the Beats, a dark-eyed romantic saint of the
underground, dedicated to living life on the fringes in an
eternal search for kicks and experience. We can see him,
standing in the Village on a Saturday night, his back against
a neon bar sign, the breast pocket of his button-down shirt
full with notebook and pencil, a sad and edgy look upon his
face. Or hear him, reading passages from his books to the
accompaniment of a jazz piano, his voice melancholy, plain-
tive, full of rhythm and blues. We may know that, until his
dying day, Kerouac lived with his mother — not exactly the
choice of a rebel angel — or that despite his celebrated boast
about writing *On The Road* in three weeks, it was only the
novel's *final draft* he completed so quickly, a draft preceded
by at least three years worth of misfires and alternate takes.
But somehow the truth — which Kerouac, to his credit, *did*
try to tell in his writing, if not always in his life — is simply
not as compelling as the myth.

Partly, that's the fault of his friends and defenders —
Ginsberg, for instance, who has, at times almost single-
handedly, tried to keep the Kerouac flame alive, or biographer Ann Charters, whose career was made by writing and
teaching about Kerouac and the Beats. Also to blame,
though, are the members of the American literary counterculture, who, for the most part — and even after all these
years — have found themselves hard-pressed to come up
with a better, more defining metaphor of what they are up to
than the figure of Kerouac himself. From Boulder, Colorado,

with its Jack Kerouac School of Disembodied Poetics, to Los Angeles, with its burgeoning neo-Beat coffeehouse/readings scene, to New York City, where not too many months before my visit to Lowell, I attended a marathon performance of *Mexico City Blues*, complete with jazz band backing and a roster of performers including Ginsberg, Herbert Huncke, and Carl Solomon — Kerouac's specter continues to haunt the underground, a ghost in its machine. And yet when all is said and done, even Ginsberg has acknowledged, "There is no longer any hope for the Salvation of America proclaimed by Jack Kerouac and others of our Beat Generation ...All we have to work from now is the vast empty quiet space of our own Consciousness."

Those are words worth paying attention to, words to keep in mind. For the 1940s and 1950s are a lifetime away, and the myths that might have sustained us once can no longer do so now. Maybe it's true, as Ann Charters writes in her introduction to the Viking Portable Library's *Portable Beat Reader*, that as "generations [move] on...[w]hat is left is the work of the writer...the work is what survives." But I can't help thinking of another image from Lowell, another image of that twentieth anniversary day. Just before dusk, my friend and I drove out to the cemetery where Kerouac was buried, intending to pay our respects. It was a chill New England evening, and, given the way things had been going, we didn't know what we would find. To our surprise, though, there was a straggly group of kids clustered at the grave. We parked nearby, watched as they shared a bottle of red wine, spilling a little into the earth whenever Kerouac's turn came around. In the middle of the pack, a tall, stocky teenager was reading from *Visions Of Cody* — "It's been so long since I've heard the sound of the Merrimack River washing over rocks in the middle of a soft summer's night..."

Windows open, we listened for a moment. Then we started up the car and drove on, leaving them behind.

JOE MAYNARD

THE THREE BEATS

"Pass the salt," Cassady grunted. But Kerouac sat across the table ignoring him, chewing lettuce from a diner salad that smelled like rice pudding, listening to Ginsberg puking in the john at the back of the dining room.

"Pass the salt, Jack."

It was strange, Kerouac was thinking, but if you concentrated, Ginsberg's puking was the only thing you could hear. The ice machine, the radio, the dishwasher, the crackling deep fryer, they all faded away into a white noise that reconstituted itself through Ginsberg's vomit.

"Jack!" Cassady shouted, "The salt!"

Kerouac snapped out of it and looked at Cassady's maniacal stare that tried unsuccessfully to bore a hole in his thick head.

"How can you eat?" Kerouac asked.

"What do you mean? He didn't get sick from food, he got sick from not eating enough food before we started drinking."

"Food? This is no food thing."

"Then pass the goddamn salt, sweet-cakes."

"Here." Kerouac said, slapping the small glass shaker on the greasy Formica, with perfect pitch resembling that of a firecracker, not too aggressive *or* subtle, just presence enough to say I'm here, fuck you. But this highly evolved percussive moment was wasted on Cassady who already was into the next moment, that of salting. He'd dressed his burger in the moment before last, and the perfect steaming burger and fries moment would soon vanish if he didn't move quick. Must sprinkle an even layer of salt while the hot grease dances on the surface of the fries. Must mix the top crust of salt crystals through the pile for even distribution with potatoes and catsup. Must take the still steaming burger in hand. Must fill mouth. Must crunch lettuce through meat. Must stuff fries into mouth while burger is still there. Must, must, must...

Kerouac watched, disgusted more with his dud of an order than with Cassady's table manners. Salad. What was he thinking? He was ripping drunk, but so what? That never impaired his judgment before. He looked at Ginsberg's turkey club, which sat regal like a castle on a mountain, two toothpicks perched on top waving shredded cellophane flags of amber and crimson. He switched plates and ate like nobody's business.

"What a hypocrite," Cassady mumbled while Kerouac stuffed his middle eye to capacity. It wasn't a pretty sight. He'd aged like hell. Thank god his mother wasn't around to see it.

Ginsberg finished vomiting and gargled in front of the mirror. His hair was in horizontal flight like Bozo the clown, but he knew he was a better poet. On the other hand, Bozo had Butchy Boy, and who did Ginsberg have? A couple of middle-aged has-beens? Although Cassady did keep his muscle tone, he smelled like vinegar, and his body was increasingly more boxed-shaped, void of presence, just thick like heavy cake. One last look in the mirror and Ginsberg marched back into the dining room like the King of Comedy.

"Salad?" he said looking at the other two, "Salad?"

"Yeah, salad," Kerouac mumbled through flying bits of turkey, tomato and mayonnaise. "That's what you ordered, isn't it?"

"No!" Ginsberg said, trying to remember exactly what he did order, "I don't eat salad!" He'd been drinking, he thought, but he wasn't drunk. Actually, after puking, he was completely sober. "Waiter!" he shouted, "I didn't order salad!"

The lanky, zit-clad Greek boy folded the sports section,

and rose from his booth by the door determined to nip this one at the bud. With his hands clasped behind his back, shoulders straight, chest out, he looked down at the three aging misfits. "You order cheeseburger, you order salad, you order turr-r-re-key club, you sweetch tur-re-key club with friend, not my fault." And with that he returned to his booth mumbling curses in Greek.

"How could you let another customer take my food!" Ginsberg shouted at the Greek. "You can't just let everybody who walks in here take each other's food! That's, that's out-rageous!"

"You don't know what you're talking about," the Greek said, not giving merit to the old drunk's rant.

But this drunk was Allen Ginsberg! And he stood up, slapped his palm on the table, and dilating his diaphragm like Pavoratti wailed, "I know EXACTLY what I'm talking about! I AM A POET! I AM THE GREAT ALLEN GINSBE-E-R-R-G!"

"Goddammit Ginsberg," Cassady gasped, "Brush your teeth before this place catches fire."

Ginsberg looked down at Cassady. His eyelids disap-peared into the back of this head. His face turned beet red. "What do YOU know you pathetic cretin!" And with that, he stuck his middle and index fingers in Cassady's nostrils, raising him from his chair. Kerouac jumped in by slapping Ginsberg and going, "Yuk, yuk, yuk." The 3 beat stooges slapped and quacked as if their inner comics had finally realized *their* moment of glory. The room was filled with drunken pandemonium, plates falling to the floor, tables turning, catsup flying, coffee spilling. The Greek panicked. Picking up a spatula from the grill, he charged the 3, swat-ting and kicking them out the door.

The 3 beats lay in a pile on the sidewalk. Their legs inter-twined like scrap metal in a junk heap. Ginsberg looked around the street. There were Gaps and Blockbusters, Pizzeria Unos and Loews quadroplexes. A T-shirt clad teenager was walking towards them, and hoping the young man would help him up, Ginsberg extended a needy hand.

"Sorry, old man," the boy said, walking by, "No change."

Ron Kolm

Man in the Grey Flannel Beret

(Thanx and a tip of the hat to Mike Golden)

I n the early 70s, I was a stoned-out hippie working in a bookstore on the Lower East Side of Manhattan. I had hair down to my butt, a peace sign dangling from a leather lanyard around my neck and a dog-eared copy of *Howl* in my back pocket.

Luckily for me, the bookstore job was pretty low key. There weren't a lot of customers—in fact, parts of the neighborhood had been burned out and almost everybody had moved away, so there wasn't much else to do *except* get high. Sometimes, on *really* slow nights, we'd close the cash register and have poetry readings.

One desultory summer evening Allen Ginsberg and Rollo Whitehead read there together. Whitehead was fantastic! He was so good it was almost *unbearable*. And Ginsberg was no slouch either. After the reading Ginsberg invited us to accompany the poets to a bar for some beers.

Man, I got so excited! I was finally going to hear firsthand those rumored stories about wild fucking in freight cars, drug crazed nights in exotic Mexican jungles and sleazy hustling on the Four-O-Deuce. I lit a joint and eagerly followed the poets across the street to the Centre Pub. But the conversation didn't go at all the way I thought it would.

Ginsberg proceeded to minutely detail for our enjoyment his book and record deals—how many tenths of a cent he got per copy of *Howl* sold. The only interesting moment occurred when Ginsberg interrupted himself to shout, "*Who the fuck is Maynard G. Krebs, anyway?*" After a couple of hours of that, I got thoroughly drunk and left, bitterly disappointed.

By the mid-'80s, I was working in a different bookstore on St. Marks Place. I had a buzz-cut, wore black leather jackets and had a tattoo on my dick. Ginsberg's *Collected Poems* had just been published in an expensive hardcover edition. To tell you the truth, I didn't give a rat's ass about his work anymore, but the bookstore was doing a brisk business in the red dustjacketed item. The first shipment rapidly sold out—so we ordered more.

The store's owner gave me Ginsberg's phone number and told me to ask him to come by and sign copies of his book. Books signed by their authors usually sell faster than unsigned ones—it's a *prestige* thing. I said ok, and when I had a spare moment, I dialed the number. Ginsberg answered—that was my first surprise—I'd expected an answering machine, or some kind of intermediary.

"Hi, Mr. Ginsberg," I said. "Is there any chance you could come by the bookstore and sign copies of your new book?"

"Sure," he said, "but only if you can tell me exactly how many copies have sold."

"I don't know," I answered truthfully, somewhat taken aback by his request.

"Well, you'd better find out," he snapped, "if you want to see me anytime in the *near future.*"

"Well, just a minute—I'll ask the boss," I said in a panic, knowing I'd be in deep shit if I fucked this up. The guy I worked for was a total anal-retentive who talked a good humanistic liberal line—but was basically just another fascist beneath the bullshit. He liked to give orders, and he loved to make money, but he really got off on thinking he was respected by the local literary heavyweights. If Ginsberg didn't show up, it'd be such a blow to his ego, he'd have me cleaning the toilet with a toothbrush for the rest of my shift.

I put my hand over the receiver and asked the other clerks if anyone knew exactly how many copies of Ginsberg's collected works we'd already sold. Nobody had a clue. I took my hand off the receiver and said, "Fifty."

"Great," he said. "I'll be right over."

Ron Sukenick

The Fifteen Minutes

At one time I thought that Allen Ginsberg was everywhere. Because everywhere I went Allen would be there—if I was in Boulder Allen was there, if I was in Paris Allen was there, if I was on Bleecker Street Allen was there, if I was in Alphabet City Allen was there, if I was on Fifth Avenue Allen was there, he was even there if I was in Brooklyn. But then I figured out what was going on: there were actually many Allen Ginsbergs, or anyway, many pieces of him. There was the mean and hungry Allen Ginsberg I encountered in the early Sixties when I tried talking to him after a demonstration and he brushed me off, there was the preoccupied in cerebration looking Allen Ginsberg I came across in the coffeeshop on Avenue B and Fourteenth Street when I saw he left his cigarettes on the counter and didn't give them back because last time he was mean and when it first struck me that Allen was less a Beat Angel than a shrewd boho saint and put him into one of my East Village stories as a character "shrewd as a saint," there was Allen Ginsberg the booming bard, there was scholar Ginsberg talking poetics in Boulder and chasing boys, there was the fame-crazed Allen Ginsberg telling me how he'd just read to a stadium audience of 20,000 (30? 40? 50,000? 100,000?), there was the warmly courteous double-taking Allen Ginsberg who suddenly recognized me as Someone in some pseudo-important milieu (like, I didn't know you would be here too Ron), there was the generous Allen promoting other deserving litworkers in his self-promotions, the statesmanlike Allen introducing me to Trungpa Rimpoche, the loyal Allen supporting old friends, the fighting for freedom Allen taking on the CIA with voluminous files, the charismatic Allen inspiring an *American Book Review* support party with appropriate words, the Allen of Ginsberg industries when you call to get the person in charge of this or that person in charge of that or the Rosenthal in charge of general affairs, there's Allen telling me he never wanted to be an outsider it's just that he was being kept out and wanted in, there's the tired and harassed and rushed Allen who's taken on more than he can handle and you worry he's going to drop like a cloak & suit exec with a bum ticker and too much to do.

Above all there's Allen Ginsberg the poet crazy, which he definitely is not. Or maybe I figure about twenty-five percent. The public image isn't the personal reality. Since Allen is a role model for many it's important to let that cat out of the bag. Crazy or shrewd, the Ginsberger can come with or without. Does he contradict himself? Yes, he contradicts himself.

Once a long time ago publishing was basically printing. Then, in our quick century it became editing, and more recently distribution. In the Sixties, with the help of new electronic technologies or a reversion to cheap and easy ones, writers were able to, as they used to say, seize the means of production and—even if in a small beginning way —distribution. But the current and maybe terminal evolution in publishing is that now it's become mainly promotion. It may turn out that Ginsberg's chief genius contribution to literary history, poetry aside, is that he was the first to seize the means of promotion.

Time was when for an undergrounder to elbow into fameville was ferociously frowned upon, considered in fact what was known as selling out. Even inadvertent fame was regarded with suspicion. While there was wisdom in this attitude in the past for various reasons, by the time the Sixties rolled around and there was a real opportunity to affect the mainstream culture in ways to one's liking, it became an outmoded stance before most subterraneans knew what was happening. It was ripe for ruin, and people like Ginsberg, Warhol and Norman Mailer quickly proceeded to ruin it. The Pop Art phase was the most obvious result.

But enough already. The pendulum, as it always does, has swung back the other way. The Allen Overkill we've all been undergoing recently is a just a symptom of this. I've had Beat Celebrations and Kerouac films up the kazoo. We've all learned from Allen, maybe too well. The real question is how do writers take control of the means of promotion—which is to say of their reputations—without going back to now corny concepts of selling out? How to make money while subverting the money machine? Has self-promotion taken precedence over the quality of production? Do we have to keep our promoscopes forever fixed on Letterman and *People* magazine?

Where promotion was, anti-promotion there shall be. The Yippies were good at it, but Yippies quickly turned to Yuppies. You can manipulate the media a little bit but not a lot. They're bigger than you and it quickly becomes a question of who is manipulating who. The short answer is to keep your tongue in your cheek or you'll find somebody else's there in short order. The long answer is develop your own network and undercut the free market mentality: whatever sells is good. The key is network loyalism. Don't worry about moving into the mass market for your fifteen minutes, or about dropping out of it. The network will support you if you support it, acting as a safety net. The network is not just the means to making it, it's the source of the values that made you. Let go of that and what have you got? Making it? Making what? Fame and fortune are great, but you can be famous and fortunate without being amnesiac and schizophrenic about where you came from and where you're heading.

Rest in peace, Allen, not in pieces.

BOB WITZ

ALLEN GINSBERG:
FROM BEATNIK TO LANDMARK

Key to Allen Ginsberg his change in dress? From black grunge tshirts jeans Uncle Sam hat to 3piece suits, wild frizzly exploding beard hair to neat trims, sneakers to ties $200 shoes, from stoned idiot clown intellectual to man of letters elder statesman.

Has he changed? Or is and was always plotting career success bigtime fame. or just late following Jerry Rubin Rubin becoming Wallstreeter incipient rightist initially imitated Ginsberg in love microphones cameras bumdress if not sex orientation. narcissism and egomania. necessary? Ginsberg jumped each new wave beats om bombs hippies vietnam yippies, flower power children community nature, India indians marxism tibet meditations, black power rage days of drugs wine and roses rage, hell's angels pop and warholism, sitins beins exorcisms levitations bombings marching protest demands, drop out tunein his asshole, rock dylan clash nuremberg type rallies, cults elitist power snobs gibberish lacerations hypnosis, blood death freak sideshows cannibalism society, torture suicide shock insanity madness, catatonic ping pong hallucinations, tenements broken glass dead professors empty lots.

Ginsberg is an American Icon. He faces every direction. The only things he skipped I guess too late are the current muscle building craze and sports mania — but wouldn't he dig taking steroids and pumping iron and the inprogress counterculture of knives razors guns xrated pornshops graffiti gangstas. Today he's much closer to his own old modern world of bullshit hype MTV movies rock business (he's still part of that and always was). hustler conman druglord.

Was he always what he is now. a conservative businessman. What's Walt to him or he to Walt Blake or whoever.

He kept all scraps of memorabilia from the smallest note and motes of dust to the mountains. What is the motive for such sustained action? Isn't it the plan for future recognition fame deification?

Biblical boy on the move, moving like the water the waves and Neal Cassady. Moses Marx John the Baptist (Lennon as Jesus) Ginsberg: a host of disciples most of whom absorbed like Rubin (kill your parents) by corporate America. Ginsberg was 1 of the first artist-politicians always campaigning to be elected.

His massive black hole ego would absorb the sun all the stars all the light all matter blotting out everything but himself and a chorus of mirrors.

LANCE OLSEN

CYBERMORPHIC
BEAT-UP GET-DOWN
SUBTERRANEAN HOMESICK
REALITY-SANDWICH BLUES

I'm a, like, poet. Mona. Mona Sausalito. I write lyrics for my boyfriend's band, Plato's Deathmetal Tumors. Plato's Deathmetal Tumors kicks butt. It's one of the best Neogoth bands in Seattle. My boyfriend's name is Mosh. Mosh shaved his head and tattooed it with rad circuitry patterns. He plays wicked cool lead and sings like Steve Tyler on amphetamines. Only that's not his real name. His real name is Marvin Goldstein. But so. Like I say, I'm a poet. I write about human sacrifices, cannibalism, vampires, and stuff. Mosh loves my work. He says we're all going to be famous some day. Only right now we're not, which bites, cuz I've been writing for like almost ten months. These things take time, I guess. Except we need some, like, cash to get by from week to week? Which is why Mosh one days says take the part-time job at Escort a la Mode. Why not? I say. Which I guess kind of brings me to my story.

See, I'm cruising Capitol Hill in one of the company's black BMWs when my car-phone rings. Escort a la Mode's a real high-class operation. Escortette's services go for $750 an hour. We usually work with foreign business types. Japs and ragheads mostly. Politicians, too. With 24 hours' notice, we can also supply bogus daughters, brothers and sons. You name it. Except there's absolutely nothing kinky here. We don't even kiss the clients. No way. Handshakes max. Take them out, show them the town, eat at a nice restaurant, listen to them yak, take them to a club, watch them try to dance, take them home. Period. We're tour guides, like. Our goal is to make people feel interesting. Therma Payne — she's my boss — Therma says our job is to "give good consort." Therma's a scream.

But so. Like I say, my car-phone rings. I answer. Dispatcher gives me an address, real chi-chi bookstore called Hard Covers down by the fish market. My client's supposed to be this big-deal writer guy who's reading there. Poet. Allen something. Supposed to have been famous back in like the Pleistocene Error or something. Worth bazillions. So important I never even heard of him. But, hey. It's work.

Now I'm not being like unmodest or anything, okay? But I happen to be fricking gorgeous. No shit. My skin's real white. I dye my hair, which is short and spiked, shoe-polish black, then streak it with these little wisps of pink. Which picks up my Lancome Corvette-red lipstick and long Estee Lauder Too-Good-To-Be-Natural black lashes. When I talk with a client, I'll keep my eyes open real wide so I always look Winona-Ryder-surprised by what he's saying. I'm 5'2", and when I wear my Number Four black-knit body-dress and glossy black Mouche army boots I become every middle-aged man's bad-little-girl wetdream. So I don't just *walk* into Hard Covers, okay? I kind, what, *sashay*. Yeah. That's it. Sashay. I've never been there before, and I'm frankly pretty fucking impressed. Place is just *humongous*. More a warehouse than a bookstore. Except that it's all mahogany and bronze and dense carpeting. Health-food bar. Espresso counter. Dweeb with bat-wing ears playing muzak at the baby grand. Area off on the side with a podium and loads of chairs for the reading. Which is already filling. Standing room only. People are real excited. And books. God. Books. Enough books to make you instantly anxious you'll never read them all, no way, no matter how hard you try, so you mind as well not.

I'm right on time. So I ask the guy at the register for the famous rich poet. He points to the storeroom. Warming up, he says. So I go on back and knock, only no one answers. I knock again. Nada. My meter's running, and I figure I mind as well earn my paycheck, so I try the knob. Door's unlocked. I open it, stick my head in, say hi. It's pretty dark, all shadows and book cartons, and the room stretches on forever, and I'm already getting bored, so I enter and close the door behind me. When my eyes adjust a little, I make out a dim light way off in a distant corner. I start weaving toward it through rows and rows of cartons. As I get closer, I can hear these voices. They sound kind of funny. Worried, like. Real fast and low. And then I see them. I see the whole thing.

Maybe five or six guys in gray business suits and ties, real like FBI or something, are huddling over this jumble on the floor. At first I don't understand what I'm looking at. Then I make out the portable gurney. And this torso on it, just this torso, naked and fleshy pink in a Barbie-doll sort of way, rib cage big as a cow's, biggest fucking belly you ever saw. Out of it are sticking these skinny white flabby legs, between them this amazingly small little purple dick and two hairy marbles. Only, thing is, the chest isn't a real chest? There's a panel in it. And the panel's open. And one of the guys is tinkering with some wiring in there. And another is rummaging through a wooden crate, coming up with an arm, plugging it into the torso, while a third guy, who's been balancing a second arm over his shoulder like a rifle or something, swings it down and locks it into place.

I may be a poet, okay, but I'm not a fucking liar or anything. I'm just telling you what I saw. Believe it or not. Go ahead. Frankly I don't give a shit. But I'm telling you, I'm standing there, hypnotized like, not sure whether to run or wet myself, when this fourth guy reaches into the crate and comes up with, I kid you not, the *head*. I swear. I fucking swear. A *head*. The thing is so gross. Pudgy. Bushy. Gray-haired. And with these *eyes*. With these sort of glazed *eyes* that're looking up into the darkness where the ceiling should've been. I could hurl just thinking about it.

Anyway, after a pretty long time fidgeting with the stuff in the chest, they prop the torso into a sitting position and start attaching the head. It's not an easy job. They fiddle and curse, and once one of them slips with a screwdriver and punctures the thing's left cheek. Only they take some flesh-toned silicon putty junk and fill up the hole, which works just fine. And the third guy reaches into his breast pocket and produces these wire-rimmed glasses, which he slips into place on this thing's face, and then they all stand back, arms folded, admiring their work and all, and then the first guy reaches behind the thing's neck and punches what must've been the ON/OFF button.

Those eyes roll down and snap into focus. Head swivels side to side. Mouth opens and close its fatty lips, testing. And then, shit, it begins *talking*. It begins fucking *talking* . *I'm with you in Rockland. I'm wuh-wuh-wuh-with you...But my agent. What sort of agent is that? What could she have been thinking? Have you seen those sales figures? A stone should have better figures than that! I'm wuh-with you in the nightmare of trade paperbacks, sudden flash of bad PR, suffering the outrageousness of weak blurbs and failing shares. Where is the breakthrough book? Where the advance? Share with me the vanity of the unsolicited manuscript! Show me the madman bum of a publicist! Movie rights! Warranties! Indemnities! I am the twelve percent royalty! I am the first five thousand copies! I am the retail and the wholesale, the overhead and the option clause! Give me the bottom line! Give me the tax break! Give me a reason to collect my rough drafts in an antennae crown of commerce! Oh, mental, mental, mental hardcover! Oh, incomplete clause! Oh, hopeless abandon of the unfulfilled contract! I am wuh-wuh-wuh-with you!...I am wuh-wuh-wuh-with you in Rockland...I am...*

"Oh, shit," says the first guy.

"Balls," says the second.

The body is a prosthesis for the mind! the famous rich poet says.

"We should've let him go," says the third guy.

"When his ticker stopped," says the first.

"When his liver quit," says the second.

"One thing," says the fourth. "Nanotech sure ain't what it's cracked up to be."

"You got that right," says the third.

Thirty thousand books in 1998 alone, the famous rich poet says, *but they couldn't afford it. Tangier, Venice, Amsterdam. What were they thinking? Wall Street is holy! The New York Stock Exchange is holy! The cosmic clause is holy! I'm wuh-wuh-wuh...I'm wuh-wuh-wuh...wuh-wuh-wuh...*

"Turn him off," says the fifth one.

Pale greenish foam begins forming on the famous rich poet's lips, dribbling down his chin, spattering his hairless chest.

"Yeah, well," says the second.

"Guess we got some tightening to do," says the third, reaching behind the thing's neck.

But just as he pressed that button, just for a fraction of an instant, the stare of the famous rich poet fell on me as I tried scrunching out of sight behind a wall of boxes. Our eyes met. His looked like those of a wrongly convicted murderer maybe like one second before the executioner throws the switch that'll send a quadrillion volts or something zizzing through his system. In them was this mixture of disillusionment, dismay, fear, and uninterrupted sorrow. I froze. He stretched his foam-filled mouth as wide as it would go, ready to bellow, ready to howl. Except the juice failed. The power paled. His mouth slowly closed again. His eyes rolled back up inside his head.

And me? I said fuck this. Fuck the books, fuck the suits, fuck Escort a la Mode, fuck the withered old pathetic shit. This whole thing's *way* too fricking rich for *my* blood.

And so I turned and walked.

NEAL CASSADY DIDN'T KNOW HOW TO DRIVE

SONG WRITTEN BY SPARROW © 1994

PERFORMED BY BLAIR WILSON #425 © 1994

JENNIFER KABAT

CAROLYN CASSADY

C arolyn buries her head in the pillow thinking of her past with Neal. The dreams and promises shatter forever. She collects his hairs from the pillow into a ball trying to hold onto him. After the phone call it all seems impossible. He said he'd be back soon. It takes a few minutes to sink in that "soon" means after the trip. He's still leaving her and the three month old baby to drive across the country for someone else's honeymoon even though they never got one—they couldn't afford it. They still can't with no money, no security, and a baby. She sobs rolling his hair through her fingers trying to conjure him up, trying to recapture that past where he convinced her that she mattered, that she was all that mattered, that she was the one. She tries to convince herself that she doesn't want him back, but she wants those reassuring feelings again, to feel whole again like she did when they shared postcard perfect visions of a future with "the rural home, the books we'd read together, the trips we'd shared, the sports we'd play, the family we'd raise in heaven."[1] Thinking about losing her dreams, makes Carolyn just start sobbing again. She hyperventilates through tears so she can take care of Cathy, but the thought of trudging through life alone with a baby just makes her start all over again.

That could be me, actually it is waiting for the phone to ring. Hours slip by 11, midnight, 2, 4 AM...I try to close my eyes against the pain to shut it out and sleep, but the silence keeps me awake and the anger returns in waves.

There is no peace. I understand Carolyn all too well as I watch my own dreams of family, forever, and a white picket fence skip away. I thought we both wanted it, but the "we" is only Carolyn and I. I can't even sort out my feelings from hers to begin writing about her husband Neal.

She writes of her life with Neal Cassady as some sort of story book romance that never quite makes it. That way of looking at their relationship fits with the social ideal of the '40s and '50s when they were married. Maybe that's why Carolyn hung on so long. At least she's from a different generation; I'm embarrassed to admit how much I want those suburban dreams. Maybe they're part of my female conditioning developing from fairy tales into romance novels and soap operas. Whatever it is, I can't let go of the picture.

Reading her book is like watching a soap opera couple who are supposed to be in love forever somehow stray from the path or knowing that the hero and heroine of a romance novel belong together even if they haven't realized it yet. Before she even met Neal, based solely on his reputation, she "was amazed to learn that there were men who actually dared live like those in books and movies."[2] He's this larger than life figure with this mythos around him like the other Beats. Neal stole cars and babes, his acts immortalized through other people's stories and reverence. He, actually all of the Beats, seem as cliched as any other American icon: cowboy, industrialist, plantation owner, whose legend is so exaggerated that they make perfect romance novel heroes.

I find all of that behavior irritating. I set out trying to write something glib about why I can't stand Cassady and his whole bravado trip of stealing cars and hearts. That and driving were his greatest skills. He tried to write and set out with plenty of good starts and ideas but ended up with *The First Third*, a book I can't even finish. He lives mostly through other's writing like *On the Road*, which itself languishes half read on my book shelf after I got bored with its juvenile antics.

Burroughs had a hard time with that behavior too. After one *On the Road* inspiring visit to his home in New Orleans, he describes Cassady as self centered and self serving, writing, "He does not even bother any longer to hide his machinations. I have the impression he lacks any clear notion of how he appears to others. Can he really think people are that dumb?"[3] But Carolyn's not the only one taken in by him. Cassady's first wife LuAnne, Allen Ginsberg and countless others keep coming back after betrayals and broken promises. I just want to shake some sense in them. Don't they get it?

Cassady's a good talker. Growing up in the flophouses of Denver, he had to be smart seductive in order to survive so he knows what to say to get his way. Granted he didn't necessarily talk about family and forever to every lover, he could read them and knew what each wanted to hear. No doubt he also believed what he told them like his pictures of forever and kids with Carolyn. Growing up so far from the promised stability of the American dream, Cassady probably longed for it, just as he must have longed for approval and love that he didn't get as a child. What better way to see it than in the faces and adoration of his lovers who were so painfully smitten?

Understanding those obvious psychological excuses for Cassady's behavior doesn't really explain his power over people. Even Burroughs was one of the "dumb" people. At the time of the above quote, he had recently been Cassady's lover. I get so irritated with Neal Cassady because that could be me in love with him. I see Cassady in the image of my lovers. I hate myself for it, just as embarrassed at the cliche image of artist that I fall for so easily as I am by my dreams of forever. Why don't I just write a romance novel set in the Lower East Side to live out my needs for stability and forever and that Cassady quality? Instead I rollover in bed and collect his hairs off the pillow, trying to forget my pain so I can actually write this piece on Neal Cassady.

1 Carolyn Cassady. *Off The Road: My Years with Cassady, Kerouac, and Ginsberg.* New York: Penguin Books, 1990, p. 27.
2 Cassady, p. 1.
3 William Burroughs to Allen Ginsberg. *The Letters of William S. Burroughs, 1945–1959,* Ed. and Intro. Oliver Harris. New York: Viking Press, p. 41.

MIKE TOPP

Holmes rf
Cassady 2b
Kerouac 1b
Ginsberg cf
Burroughs 3b
Huncke lf
Snyder c
Ferlinghetti ss
McClure p

DAVID HUBERMAN

THE KING

Springtime in N.Y.C. There's nothing quite like it. Walking down Avenue A with a sweet evening breeze in the air made it a beautiful night to hang out. About five of us from our group would usually follow the Friday meeting with a ritual of food and coffee. The diet of a drug addict is never a nutritious one. Addicts in recovery do not fare much better. On this night we picked one of the Polish restaurants to eat and talk because it was cheap and had the "greasy spoon" atmosphere. It sure beat White Castles. We went to the Odessa. We took a table near the window to watch the theatre of life. Swan came along with us; a nice Jewish boy who at one time had a $200-a-day heroin habit. Now he was two years clean. Gaunt-looking with yellow rotting teeth. I suspected him of being a paranoid-schizophrenic. Sporting a Bobby Darin hairstyle, he always carried the latest issue of *The Wall Street Journal* wherever he went. The guy was constantly talking about the stock market or economics. Everything came back to these two subjects. If the discussion was sex, he would bring up that he'd invested heavily in condom companies. He was the type that would talk your ear off while guzzling down an endless amount of black coffee. His cup was always bottomless.

That night our group consisted of Swan, C.C., Thursday the girl-boy, Leroy, Little John and me. A distinctive crowd if there ever was one. We were all caught up in a heated discussion about whether the Rolling Stones still counted in the nineties. C.C., an ex-topless dancer and a Stones freak, was arguing with Thursday the girl-boy. C.C. (we never knew her real name) still had a great ass for a woman in her late 30s. She had a long frosted pre-seventies haircut. A fake blond. Thursday, on the other hand, looked like she could have played for the New York Jets, except she had a feminine face and two huge knockers thanks to Mr. Silicon. We tried never to question Thursday's sexual identity. Since we were all in recovery, we respected each other and tried not to be judgmental. We were all crazy or unmanageable in one form or another. We applied the motto, "Live and let live."

"The Stones are a bunch of Republicans," Thursday kept repeating. "They sold out years ago, especially Mr. Big Lips, Mick Jagger. They don't care a hoot about their fans. All they care about is money."

"That's not true!" C.C. shouted. "They're still the greatest rock band in the world. Speed metal and rap — you call that music? It's noise, man, noise! The Rolling Stones — God bless them, man. They're still great."

"*Were* great," Thursday said. "They're a bunch of rich old queens who couldn't care less about the working class. Fuck them!"

Leroy, a six-foot-tall black man who looked a lot like Richard Pryor and had the same habit of smoking cocaine, saw his chance to stick his two cents in, "Thursday's right," he said, "Prick Jagger's just another white boy who stole everything he knows from the black man. He stole his lifestyle from the Godfather of Soul, James Brown. The boy took his music and his dance steps. What he didn't steal from James Brown, he stole from Tina Turner. He even has Tina Turner's big dick-sucking lips."

"You're full of shit," C.C. said.

"I know I am," Leroy said. "But guess what: so's Mick Jagger. And you can tell that scrawny-ass Keith Richards to sit his ass down with us."

"Well, I think Mick Jagger knows what he's doing," Little John piped in. Little John had just come back from a slip. In recovery terms, a slip is when an addict uses briefly and comes back to the program. Little John was a short but well-built Puerto Rican guy in his late 30s. He was a Vietnam vet who worked for the city as a male nurse. His favorite drug was morphine, which was easily available to him since he worked in a hospital. "The way I see it, Mick Jagger and the Stones made great music, a ton of money, and fucked the best-looking women in the world. I see nothing wrong with that."

"Well," Swan said. "That's the most intelligent thing that ever came out of your mouth. The Stones are good for the economy. Imagine where all the T-shirt schmucks would be without groups like the Stones. The Stones are big business and they are good for everybody. Whether Mick Jagger sucks dick or hangs out with the Queen of England is totally irrelevant."

"You have quite a different slant on the world," I told Swan.

"Hey — look who just walked in! Isn't that the writer who wrote that book about junkies?" Swan asked.

A skinny old man had walked into the restaurant. He had little beady eyes like a rodent and had that beaten-down look. Yet there was something youthful in his face. Then there was that decadent smile that looked totally false as if it was pasted on.

"Hey," Leroy said. "Where did that old vampire come from!"

"He looks like Bela Lugosi!" said C.C.

"More like Nosferatu," said Swan.

"I don't think that's William Burroughs. Doesn't Burroughs wear glasses?" said Thursday.

Finally I broke my silence. "That's not Burroughs. That's Herbert Huncke, the guy who inspired Burroughs. He's the King."

"The King of what?" Leroy wanted to know.

"The King of Junkies," I said. "This guy has been around since the forties. He used to hang around Times Square and roll drunks and do petty crimes. He was in and out of jail for years. I hear he still shoots junk and he looks like he's on a mission right now."

No one but our table seemed to notice the old man. He was invisible to the other patrons. He wore an old gray overcoat. It was dirty and disheveled, yet it somehow reminded me of wings. He paused at our table, gave us this thin junkie smile and nodded, but before anyone could say anything he had made it to the bathroom door.

"That's the oldest dope fiend I've ever seen," said Leroy. "Cat gotta be in his late 60s and still shooting dope. Shit."

"You don't suppose he's just taking a dump in there, do you?" C.C. asked.

"No way — that old dope fiend just copped. He's probably shooting a bundle in there," Leroy replied.

"Hey, you think he knows we're in recovery?" Little John asked.

"No way," Swan said. "He probably stopped at our table because he subconsciously recognized us for what we are."

"*Were*," corrected Thursday.

"Hey," Swan said, "how long has he been in there?"

"Over twelve minutes," I said.

"That ain't no dump. We got us a live active dope fiend in there," Leroy said.

"Could be a methadone dump," I said.

"No way," Leroy said. "His funk would have reached our table by now."

"Yeah," said Thursday, "the whole restaurant would've stunk up by now."

"Just positive thinking," I said.

Then, before anyone could get another word in, the old man walked out of the bathroom. Hunched over, on the nod, he walked quietly out of the restaurant. No one seemed to notice other than our table. We all got up simultaneously and ran to the bathroom. Leroy got there first.

"Just what I thought," Leroy said. "Shot plenty of dope in here. Left his cotton behind as a souvenir."

"The King," I said.

"Yeah, the King of the motherfucken dope fiends," Leroy said.

"Endurance, tradition, history, survival — a legend; that's how kings are made," Swan said.

JIM KNIPFEL

HUMAN, ALL TOO (ALMOST) HUMAN

I n 1991, I believe it was, the folks at Blast Books released a small anthology entitled *The Drug User*, which was a collection of short pieces by, well, *drug users*, all of them written before 1960. Good little collection. To celebrate the book's release, Tower Books sponsored a reading at their store in lower Manhattan. The featured reader (quite likely because none of the other contributors were alive) was going to be none other than Herbert Huncke, beat legend.

My then-wife Laura and I showed up for the festivities. We were still reasonably new in town and pretty much the only people we knew were the folks at Blast. It seemed like a good excuse to get out of Brooklyn for an evening.

We hung out near the back of the space that was set up for the reading and surveyed the crowd.

"Jesus Christ," I whispered to Laura, "put out a book about drugs and you end up attracting every hipster junkie in New York."

It was true. We were surrounded by skinny, cadaverous, dead-eyed, leather-jacketed punk rock types. They swarmed like a crowd of thick flies — well, very slow-moving flies at least — around the chairs and down the aisles.

"D'jya ever notice," I whispered to her again, "that if a junkie makes it past the age of 30, they inevitably end up looking exactly like William Burroughs? I mean, look around you." I made a sweeping gesture, taking in the whole crowd. "*Look* at these people — look at the faces — regardless of the hair or the clothes or whatever — all these people look just like William Burroughs."

That was true, too. It was a very strange phenomenon.

"I mean, look at the old woman over there—" I pointed a little too obviously, "—even that old woman looks just like William Burroughs!"

Laura shot a sharp elbow into my ribs. "You idiot — that's *Herbert Huncke!*"

I was sitting in The Big Ten Bar in Minneapolis, talking to an English fellow, both of us well on our way towards oblivion. Only interesting thing about the Big Ten was the bathroom. I've never seen this replicated in any other bar. Instead of a normal couple of urinals tucked along the wall, they just had a big *bathtub* in the middle of the floor. You just chose a spot and pissed into this bathtub. It was very odd.

So I'm talking to this British guy — I forget his name, not even sure if ever knew it — and it turns out that he went to college at the University of Kansas in Lawrence.

"Yeah, Burroughs, he was everywhere," he told me, without any provocation. "At first I thought it was amazing, y'know, '*My God, there's William Burroughs!*' But after a while, it was just like, *nothing.* You'd be in a grocery store, and there he'd be again, there's Burroughs buying grapefruit."

"Grapefruit?"

"Yeah, he was always buying grapefruit. Nothing else. But 90 percent of the time when you'd see him, he'd just be shuffling down the street with his cane, carrying this clear plastic shopping bag."

"Uh-huh."

"And you know what was in it?"

"Grapefruit?"

"Nope."

"Then I've no idea."

"A bottle of vodka. That's all. All the time. A clear plastic bag with a bottle of vodka in it, just shuffling down the street."

"I'm not sure why, but that's very funny."

That's all the British fellow had to say about Burroughs.

CAROL WIERZBICKI

ADDING MACHINES, GUNS AND HEREDITY

(A Perot infomercial)

I 'd like to take a moment to talk about the real William S. Burroughs. You might not even know who he is, so let me tell you about him.

Now the way these literary critics and pop culture gurus are painting him, he's some kind of messiah who redeemed language. He's an icon who saved corporate-dominated America from itself.

Let me show you this chart. As you can see, Billy comes from honorable roots. With Robert E. Lee's descendants on one side, and the brilliant Burroughs inventors and mechanics on the other, Billy pretty much had success in the bag.

His maternal grandfather, James Wideman Lee, was a Bible-thumping preacher, and his maternal grandmother, Eufala, was active in the Women's Temperance Union. She was a tough bird and would stick a fork in any child's hand whose table manners she found wanting.

His paternal grandfather, William Seward Burroughs, invented the adding machine, making the family fortune. And his grandfather's father, Edmund, was also a mechanic and inventor, although he never bothered to get a patent on anything.

But his uncle, Ivy Lee, was a PR man who used his preacher roots to make the robber barons look like nice guys. Nothing wrong with that, if he had kept things in perspective. Too bad he had to go after bigger fish. Namely, Hitler. Ivy realized too late that the Third Reich was not Standard Oil.

Billy's mother, Laura Lee, was not that religious, but was psychic. She had a sixth sense about people, who could be trusted and who should be chucked in the trash. She adored Billy.

Billy's father, Mortimer, handled sales for the Burroughs company in Detroit, then moved the family to St. Louis to start a plate glass business. That he was an atheist did not detract from his generosity and good business sense. In a rare moment of warmth between him and Billy, he said, "There was a little dog, and his name was Rover, and he was dead, he was dead all over. That's what happens when you die."

Well, Billy went to all the best schools, had all the advantages in life, but unlike his industrious brother Mort, he threw it all away. Instead of applying himself in school and learning teamwork — something I myself value — he wasted his time on smutty dime novels like *You Can't Win*, a tale of thievery and drug abuse, and mooning over other boys. To make matters worse, there were always Irish and Welsh cooks and maids about; they taught him witchcraft.

Somewhere along the line Billy got the idea that he had to redeem the sins of his forefathers. Both his grandfather and his uncle had capitalized on their twisting of the language to serve their own ends. He got this bee in his bonnet that this was wrong, and he would somehow right it. Through his writing. He would shatter conventional narrative and undermine language and capitalism as we knew it back in the good old days, and transform both so that they would never be the same again.

Here is another chart. It shows the average annual income of a white middle class male head of a nuclear family in 1945. Pretty impressive, wasn't it. Those good old days are no more, thanks to our pal Wm. S. Burroughs. Since 1953, when his novel *Junky* appeared, the per capita income of those same middle class families has fallen by 2/3. That's 2/3 of our hard earned income, America—down the proverbial tubes.

Now, it doesn't take a rocket scientist to figure out that you can draw parallels between Burroughs's rise as a literary figure and the decline of capitalism and our language as we know and love it. As the great Allen Ginsberg once pointed out, "Without free trade, how could publishing exist?"

You're smart, America. And you don't need me to tell you that with crap like *Junky* and *Naked Lunch*, Billy was just getting back at his parents and relatives. He just could not bring himself to forgive his Uncle Ivy for loving capitalism not wisely, but too well. Or the rest of his family for being successful. He could not have dreamed at the time that with his foul behavior and writing he was destroying all the structures that this country was built upon, that made us truly great, that made us want to pull together. He knocked down capitalism as surely as he crunched sentences. Haven't you asked yourself about the coincidence of our language being corrupted at around the same time the dollar began to lose its value at breakneck pace?

Well, I say to you, Billy, grow up. Dust that magic powder off your snakeskin boots, and go home. The only honest job you ever held was an exterminator's job. You should have stuck with that; you were good at killing things. You knocked down the pillars on which this great nation was built and left us a world we would not want to leave to our children, much less our pets.

America, I want you to go over to your bookshelves right now and pull out all the Burroughs and make a nice bonfire out of him. Then go out tomorrow to the closest bookstore and get yourself some nice positive writer like Barbara Taylor Bradford or Robert Fulghum. Then we can talk about restoring our beloved country to what it was before this disease started corroding it. We can do it. You can and I can together. Thank you, America. I love you. Goodnight.

JILL S. RAPAPORT

WON'T YOU GO HOME BILL BURROUGHS

B urroughs trashed the wife because her head was bigger than the apple he was aiming for in a late-century rerouting of ancient masculine instinct, the destruction of the mother goddess and reformation of the patrilineal, which in turn enhanced an already inescapable putrefaction, the decay of homo sapiens.

She was boring, faceless like the little female fetuses with which the biblically obsessed component of Aryan Nation has begun doing business, the better to guilt-trip the young and pregnant. She couldn't stand up to him. Humanity is united in its hatred of wives and mothers. Women have to answer in manly terms or get trashed in shooting accidents like the william tell overture. It is explained in language like this: "Of course, Burroughs hates women." Got news for ya dad. All men do.

Burroughs has been panned by Americans as a dame-hating homo, which neatly lets straights off the hook of the entrenched misogyny with the pit bull bite on the balls of dominant culture as it is now constructed, a wretched little phenomenon located somewhere behind the compost heap of sugarcane creationism and worse unless, of course, you get something out of it, and some of us do.

Tell ya sumpn else. AIDS in Zaire is boring. Famous people are boring. Murder is boring. Nobody can take it anymore.

What is it to me who loved Ginsberg or bone-jumped him or why? It bores me. I'd shoot him easy. Yes, I think I would, in a game of William Tell. Shoot everybody else that bores or scares me too. Redneck Euro-derived crackers in small Alabama towns and Cradle of Humanity-derived brats with gold teeth dreaming of bashing in my white skull on the train to Coney Island.

Guns are boring, except when they're not. Women dream of guns, and it is this which separates them from the mythical depictions of themselves, divided, unable to fire, domestic right down to the black rings around their burners. Men are the enemy, and anybody who says they are not is paid off, stupid, or has a death wish. But you could, ideally, get along with a man. Women, on the other hand, like any other oppressed group, are annoying. They're a bore. Yeah I'm one, what of it?

I'd a shot her too.

Hey I used to hate old people till I got old. Now I hate the young.

Hate the Chairman of the Board of Union Carbide, Ronald Reagan and the Pope but I hate anybody beating down the gates of white privilege too, since I hate giving up any of the meager goodies I got.

The family and the church, and gay guys not inviting me into their dick bars, not seeing me when I move tall between them and the objects of their teste-heavy lust. I hate all of 'em.

I think it was Natalie Wood who said, "Now I too have hate."

I enjoyed the first two paragraphs of *Naked Lunch*, which is about all I've had time for. He hates women, he is the enemy, but he hates men too. Anyway, he's only one guy, skinny and old. The greater part of the world doesn't give a shit. Misanthropy pales beside misogyny. Its inclusivity excludes exclusivity. I think it was Mercedes McCambridge who said that.

And good books or bad yeah I'd shoot him too, claiming it was a game, which in this case wouldn't be lying.

Hatred is an underexamined and overmystified force which makes for some pretty bad structures.

Like Laocoon on some militarily vast scale you consume whole what won't have you and it turns your insides black.

William Burroughs shot the bitch because he was the bitch. He aborted her, which is no more nor less than that which all men have always wanted to do to all women, just as women have always wanted to do it to them. He fired first, before she was ready to fire on him. That's all. Nobody could have prevented it. It was an act that in the absence of that sentimental scandal known as judeo-christian morality could be seen as the culmination of the decree of an oracle or a random movement of molecules in space, without cause or effect. What are guns for, if not shooting? The real crime is interpretation.

William Burroughs has said that the shooting was an accident. Who is anyone to deny or second-guess such drooling baloney? What happens happens. If women would get out of the way they'd get shot less often. If they'd stop unilaterally holding up the battered body of civilization maybe we could get on with the business of recovering our savage origins and start over again, at year zero, where nobody carries weight and everybody lives in harmony, killing their attackers first-hand.

He was tired of her cooking breakfast for him, tired of putting his arm around her in that tired old patriarchal manner.

He was tired of being a man, and if she had been equally tired, it would have been him lying on the floor and her writing the books and making appearances.

Divorce, drugs and disengagement were, for the white goddess, the three wild and mopheaded sisters of the lexical wood endowed by Dionysus at that magic crossroads of splendor and mortality, where the human project peaked and started upon its downward journey.

William Burroughs had a son, William Burroughs, Jr. The son wrote a book and died. One son, one son's book, was enough. Having fathered that, the idea of wife was no longer more vibrant than the idea of yesterday's hypodermic needle, yesterday's toast or yesterday's holy underwear. William Burroughs fired the wife. Enough was enough. And now William Burroughs, husband and father, was laid to rest.

Every man needs to be penetrated and every woman needs a wife, a gun, and the balls to shoot them both.

In this modern land, fatigue is death, which is why you don't want anybody getting tired of you, because the only weapon against fatigue is a gun. If we as a nation could get tired together, and pull triggers together, everything would certainly be all right.

Like I care one way or the other...

CLAUDE TAYLOR

A WALK ON THE WILDE SIDE

M aybe three years ago, I was walking down twenty-third street. A fine cloudless October afternoon. I passed him in neutral speed, almost didn't notice. But it was him, and what struck me immediately was how little he had changed. Herbert Huncke—the gnarled gnome of forty-second street beatsterism. There were the photos, mostly from the early sixties, black and white and faded. Here he was now, thirty years later and hardly looking any older. I mean, here was a man who in his late twenties looked like a man in his late forties. And now here he was almost forty years later looking like a man in his mid fifties. He seemed to have aged one year or so per decade. How had it happened. I'm forty five years old. At his rate, in five years we might both appear to be the same age. In ten years I would look older than him. This was a mystery to me, and strangely disturbing too.

Ponder the imponderable. Penetrate the impenetrable. How had this aged gay junkie who looked almost twice his age forty years ago come to look almost half his age now?

Several years ago, I was invited to a party for William Burroughs on the publication of a recent book. It was at a large dark low ceilinged club on the upper east side. The place was packed with a rather raucous crowd of young pseudo-junkies, but Burroughs, himself, sitting in the midst of it all was preternaturally calm. Elegantly dressed in suit and tie, he was slim and fit, and again it struck me, How had this man, this aging gay junkie, who again had looked maybe fifty when he was twenty five, how had he managed to age so little over the course of the last forty years. Here he was, deep into his seventieth decade, and yet looked not much older than he had on the dust jacket of *Naked Lunch* circa 1959.

And so we face the question, how had the aging process, which seemed so accelerated for the first thirty years of their lives, managed to slow down so remarkably during the past forty years? There's no simple solution here and, needless to say, no one is talking. Is it a Faustian thing? Or say something along the lines of Dorian Gray? Behind a wall in some secret bedroom, is there a portrait aging horribly? A bubbling putrescence of nihilistic oils painted by Beelzebub himself?

I subscribe to the metabolic theory. Like the song says:

> Just a spoonful of semen
> Helps the heroin go down, son
> Heroin go down
> Heroin go down

Horsemen pass by.

Lawrence Fishberg

The Thing

I was having a slice in a small pizza joint near Avenue B.
"Can I have some pepper for this?"
"All out," the guy behind the counter grunted.

I noticed the pepper container near the oven, but I let it go. I was hungry and I didn't want an argument. It was an off-hour, it was pouring outside, I was the only person in this place and I figured it was wise to remain silent.

I was looking around when I noticed an old, grimy picture hanging on the wall just above the cash register. I swore it looked like a picture of William Burroughs standing next to another man I could not identify.

"That's Burroughs, isn't it?"

"Yeah," he answered, not bothering to turn around to look at the snapshot. "It was taken in Morocco."

"Who is the other guy?" I asked, very intrigued at this point.

"That's me in the picture pal," he answered angrily. "Let me tell you something, because I sell pizza to people like you doesn't mean that I haven't had a life outside of this place." He paused and looked right into my eyes. "You remind me of my cousin Billy, tall, skinny, with a long nose that looks like a dick." He let out a huge laugh.

"You're the cousin of William Burroughs?" I asked, ignoring his insult.

He let loose a tremendous fart and smiled. A number of his teeth were missing.

"It's been quite a long time since this picture was taken, dick-nose. Quite a lot of garbage under the old bridge," he said, wiping his hands on the T-shirt covering his ample stomach. "That's a dollar-seventy-five for the slice."

Being a huge Burroughs' fan, I was naturally beside myself.

"I'm a member of a group of poets called the 'Unbearables,'" I stuttered, my hand shaking as I handed him the money. "It would be great if I could have an interview with you, there are so many questions..."

"There's nothing to say, asshole," he said, cutting me off. "He's my cousin. Big deal. Whenever he's in town, he comes in here and orders a slice just like you." His eyes began to narrow and he grinned. "I bet you can shoot quite a load through that nose. Maybe I should call old Billy-Boy and you two can have a nostril-jerk contest." He howled at that one.

I felt like a character in the nineteen fifties movie *The Thing*. In the final scene these soldiers trap the monster and are about to kill him when this scientist breaks out of the crowd, runs up to the monster and begs him to share with the scientist his great "knowledge." The monster unceremoniously swats him aside.

One shouldn't be looking for words on a blank sheet of paper.

"We have a special on the menu everyday at around noon, cum-nose!" he yelled as I was walking out the door. "It's called Naked Lunch!"

I've tasted better pizza.

MARY LEARY

THE SOFT BOYS

The Soft Boys will
buy your books by the
cartload,
calling them
great literature
while the
Serpent smiles and hisses out
new words to set
cold dicks
to dreaming.

Kerouac, Burroughs and Cassady up to no good somewhere in the Midwest, circa 1962. (Note stolen bronze casting of Ballantine Ale bottle by Jasper Johns in gas tank; Kerouac draws a bead on the second ale bottle.)

HAL SIROWITZ

FOGGY WINDOWS

When I was in college, a woman that I liked told me that my work reminded her of Gregory Corso. That made me like him even more. So years later when a friend told me that she was arranging for me to read with Gregory, I was delighted. I didn't expect to get discovered. I just thought it'd be nice to meet him. But, for me, meeting him was a little like a young boxer finally getting the chance to talk to Muhammed Ali, & discovering that he was punch drunk, & had trouble talking. I met Gregory, but he wasn't really there.

We were in the same car going to the poetry reading. I sat in the back seat. She introduced him to me, but he wasn't very talkative. In fact, he said nothing to me. Then five minutes later he asked her who was the person sitting in the back. She introduced me to him again, but this time he said too much. He wanted to know why I didn't take the bus.

She told him that she had to stop for gas. He told her that first he had to do something. He made her stop at a liquor store. He bought a pint of J&B Scotch. We watched him fuel up. He only took small sips, but it had the same effect on him as if he had drunk the whole bottle in one gulp.

When I was little I made believe I was a car, & water was gasoline. I tried to drink a gallon's worth. I spent the night traveling between my bed & the bathroom. Gregory kept telling her to go faster, because he had to use the bathroom.

He fell asleep. She said that he was suffering from jet lag. He had just flown from California to be with her. But I've spent enough time around alcoholics & junkies to know that this wasn't jet lag. He was totally wasted.

He woke up, & said it was cold. He turned the heater all the way up. The windows started to fog. I began to sweat.

She asked him why he treated her so badly the last time that they met. He said it must have been because he was high. She disagreed, & said that she felt he was still mad at her.

I wasn't supposed to be listening. I was supposed to pretend that I wasn't there. For most of my life I've felt invisible. When I was around a crowd of people I'd have fantasies of being famous, so people would notice me, and here I was with someone famous. But if people were noticing him, he certainly wasn't noticing them.

He said that he admired Madame Blavatsky & Aleistair Crowley. He felt that they were very lucky people, because they got out of this life while they were still alive. That's what he wanted to do. He said that if you wait until your body is decayed, you may never leave.

MICHAEL CARTER

OFF BEATS CORSO

With the notable exceptions of Cassady and Huncke, who were poor pros(e), Corso stands tall as the greatest criminal poet of the Beats; his juvenile crimes are recorded somewhere in City Hall; his crimes against the polite society of '50s New York and San Fran chronicled by Kerouac under the moniker Raphael Arso — I mean Ursehole; his crimes against poetry can be found in all his books and readings (tho these be few compared with many beats and wannabeats); and his crimes against the wishes of any and all in the room (especially when drunk), continual; in fact that's what's most amazing of all his crimes, that they just keep continuing, like a Sing-Sing canary that won't shut up...

The crimes here documented constitute but a paltry footnote to his manifold penal and poetical calamities; however, let the record show: I first met Corso at CBs 313, at a Richard Hell book or birthday party. Somebody said, "He's that old guy that looks like a bum over there," and sycophantic publisher that I sometimes must play, decided to introduce myself (same way I'd introduced myself to Burroughs five years before): "You're Gregory Corso?" (Blank stare) "I'm Michael Carter and I publish Redtape magazine — uh, I know your friend so-and-so." (Another blank stare which obviously meant "So?") I'd heard about his legendary temper, 'specially when soused, and digging his winetight redrimmed eyes, beat a hasty retreat.

About a year later I was finishing up the TRAGICOMIX ish; I try to do *Redtape* like a mosaic where one piece blurts into another 'n I was running Mike Golden's original Unbearable Beatnik piece where he talks about some encounter with the 'real' Gregory in the loo at St. Marks, so one afternoon hungover to hell it hit me: why not follow that with something by the real Gregory hisself? Besides, the whole issue had a kind of post/neo-beat street feel, 'n I already had stuff by Beat fellow travelers like Rattray and Sanders (plus, *Peau Sensible* had done up some Huncke, so — ugh — Corso could one up 'em). So, I called my 'friend' — just a supportive acquaintance, really — to try'n track down this elusive Urso-bear...

"Do you know where Gregory is? Do you think he'd give something for my mag?" — The line went blank a minute; "Yyeaah — who's this?" a crotchety voice growled back...I explained as best I could with precision and humility... "Fifty bucks," Corso said, "You gotta give me fifty bucks or I'm not interested." I knew I didn't have fifty bucks, but I wanted a poem, because whatever else he is, Corso's a great poet — and I *thought* it would sell magazines..."Uh, I don't got it right now...I can get it to you in a week or so." Corso: "That's what they all say; I'm a sick man — I don't feel very well; I need it now. If you can't give me the fifty bucks, I can't even talk to you" — And the line went dead...In my delirious and fevered redtape mind, I sensed a great chance to become an op. cit. in the grand an(n)als of beatdom, it was my destiny.

I knew then I had to get the fifty bucks, 'n called a few friends: nothing, nothing, nothing, "Are you kidding?" "Fuck you!" Finally an artist down the road said "O.K."; he'd never heard of Corso and didn't care...I called Gregory back up, got the address. My "friend' answered the door, "He's sleeping — here's his latest book. It's only been printed in England" (or was it English, I can't remember...) "There's a lot of previously unpublished stuff, I'm sure he'll let you publish what you want." I gave him the fifty and some old *Redtapes*. "Come back at six, he should be up by then." I called back at six, only to hear he'd went out somewhere with Allen, but had thanked me for the cash, and said he'd meet me at a nearby corner bar at noon next day...

Knowing Corso's crooked rep I was naturally apprehensive, especially when he hadn't shown nearly an hour later, but I trusted my friend, knowing him to be kind and honorable...And Gregory did show a few minutes later. "You Michael Carter? Hi, I'm Gregory." We ordered a couple of beers and sat down. He was very polite, and though his general appearance was kind of run-down (and mine usually isn't?), there was a sparkle of clarity about him, and of worldly wisdom, as he slowly explained he only had rights to one poem in the book — which happened to be about 30 pages long, though much of it too sparkled. I realized I had been slightly conned, yet went through with it, eventually micro-double columning the damn thing down to ten. Gazing hawk-like over his reading glasses, he dwelt upon the words in the book with what seemed a true poet's concern, excising a whole page about horses, "never liked that stuff about horses," he kept repeating with a grimace, and crossed out "motherfucker." "Everybody says `motherfucker' these days — doesn't mean anything."

After I'd put the mag to rest, I found out there already was an American version of the poem — and while I could claim this was the "corrected" one, wondered silently how many other versions might be out there...After publication, I delivered some copies to Gregory and his friend, and he kindly signed a few for me to give away or sell — when I took a couple to Academy books, they offered me less than the cover price...

Next time I saw Corso was at a big Beat beatoff uptown... Gregory was already in fine form, barely held in tow by Allen and some other friends. I gave Allen a copy of *Redtape* and he said Gregory'd read from it in his (Allen's) class, 'n congrats. The Urso himself was blasted and scheduled to read soon (he'd already scrawled his little epigrams all over the chalkboard; "A star/is as far/as the eye/can see/and/as near/as my eye/is to me"). The reading went fine, not too long, and it was the first time I'd heard him read live. Later, he wanted another beer and I offered to go, as one of his friends had offered to pay and I was quite thirsty too. When I returned he was really getting going — chatting up some chick, scurrilous to everyone else — Allen off to the side with that watchful look of his. I handed Corso a beer and responded to some bad joke of his, then he turned on me, with some crack about "asslicking lovers of poets"; I winced, then responded, "Poetry, Gregory, not poets..."

I last saw him at Burroughs' book-signing circus at Cooper Square. He was peeved no one was paying much mind to him. "Why does Bill get all the attention; why can't I sign some of *my* books?" and pulled a copy of *Long Live Man* off the shelf, "See this," he said pointing to the galaxy-like milky splotch on the cover — "See *this*, this was *my* cum —thirty years ago, *my* cum..." (never mind it was credited to the Palomar observatory...)

In other words, just another crime against publishing, just another beatoff crime.

C.F. ROBERTS

THE OLD BEAT POET SPEAKS

The old Beat poet hugged the coffee bar as if he was a captain steadying the wheel of his rickety tugboat. A cigarette was dangling form his lip, but my opinion is that it should have been a corncob pipe.

"Whaddya think of the kid up there, doing his rewrite of *Howl*?" he asked. "Ah, they all do it eventually, the kids. They all do a rewrite of *Howl*. Trouble is, they saturate it with four-letter words. Come to think, I've always had a kind of spiritual warfare going with Allen because his work is riddled with obscene language...he seems to be getting away from it, now...seems almost — gentrified...in the finer sense of the word, I mean. He knows he's getting up there in years...doesn't want his legacy to be a bunch of four-letter words, you know?"

He took a long drag off his cigarette — "So, what do you like, kid? You like Bukowski? You look like a Bukowski guy... I've worked with him...he's good, but don't be fooled — he really doesn't live like he writes; he isn't always drunk, he doesn't spend all his time at the track...how about Eliot? You like Eliot? Yeah, good ole T.S..."

He went on and on. He had an illustrious resume behind him...poems, mostly, but also short stories, essays, critical pieces—he'd appeared in every damn journal with the word "Review" tacked onto the end of it, a feat which has eluded me to this day.

"Y'know, kid, that magazine you do...I don't know that I would ever put any of my work in it. It's too...angry. Everything you run is so angry...I guess when you get to be my age, you get to see all sides of things.

"Yeah, I followed Kerouac after I got out of college...saw him read on Steve Allen and everything.

"Good reading tonight...lots of kids with talent. Yeah... when you get to be my age, you really don't get excited about readings, anymore...

"So, how did you ever get Lyn Lifshin to submit to your magazine? Whose arm did you twist? I did a workshop with her in upstate New York back in, I think, '86, or so...and that other one...whatsername? Girl from Ohio. Redhead. Nice girl...does a poetry journal. Met her at a book fair, once. Nice girl. How did you ever get her to submit to this rag?

"You're awfully angry kid...you ought to check out Alexander Pope. There was a poet who had it all—irony, outrage, satire...and all in rhymed couplets...

"Ever read any Adrienne Rich? Yeah, I worked with her... worked with Sylvia, too — you like Sylvia? Yeah, Poor Sylvia — her trouble was she never got over her father's death..."

He didn't say much after that. He sort of disturbed me...I don't know why.

DARIUS JAMES

BEAT CRIMESTOPPER #666: "THE COMMODE IN YOUR LIVINGROOM"

On the screen of a black & white Motorola, as bongos pound furiously in the background, a goateed Maynard G. Krebbs is shown in extreme, fish-eyed CLOSE UP. His eyes are glazed, blood shot. His lips are curled into an angry Elvis snarl. He curses Eisenhower. Vows Nixon's gift pooch Checkers will be on his plate by dinner time.

Thrusting his scrub-growth chin at the camera, he holds up a Polaroid snapshot of Joe McCarthy naked and on his knees, parting the halves of his pale and hairy hindpots. His Vaselined rectum ready to recieve a wooden dildo carved into a likeness of Joe Stalin. The dildo is strapped to the waist of a reptilian Roy Cohn.

The snapshot flutters from his fingers and the camera TILTS DOWN to his waist. Maynard unbuckles his trousers, turns and, in TIGHT CLOSE-UP, three cylindrical turds squeeze from his dilated rectum.

He wipes with a one-hundred dollar bill. "You get what you pay for" he says, walking OUT OF VIEW.

Di Prima: Ms. Fifty-Five

*O*ff-White Screen. Crawl In Black: "The road is the universal tomb, not the image of my freedom."
— René Daumal, *L'Evidence Absurde*

FADE IN. A West Village flat, conspicuously unfurnished, with white walls, a wooden floor painted gray, and an open window overlooking Hudson Street. A bare mattress on frame and springs rests against the far wall. Scotch-taped above the mattress, a print of a Monet redundancy in Saniflush blue dangles and flaps. Periodically, a breeze rattles the window-glass. The clarity of the sunlight, and the wind-swept appearance of objects and people in the room, suggest a warm, balmy afternoon at the end of spring. The bed sags slightly under the weight of its occupants. DI PRIMA, a plump, withdrawn twenty-one-year-old mute who boldly expresses shyness in the language of locked ankles and intertwined limbs, lies huddled next to IVAN, a lanky, working class Austrian expatriate of nineteen. FADE OUT.

DI PRIMA
(V.O.)
(Black Screen.) When I was seventeen and hungry, the whole world seemed too dead to hold my interest. Days passed before I knew I was even alive. By the time I met NEAL CASSADY, I had nothing to hope for but the attention I thought I'd never get. (DISSOLVE *to white.)* NEAL changed all that.
(SERIES OF STILL SHOTS *showing an idyllic diner-booth*

meeting: DI PRIMA in front of her empty plate, charmed; CASSADY, clowning with sandwich; waitress in bg. wearily scowling.)

Slick, drunk and reeking, NEAL found me dabbing my eyes at the Tiffany Diner. He told me I was Mary Magdalen. Suckered, I gave him my address.

(LAST SHOT: *CASSADY facing DI PRIMA with serious gaze, hands clasping her shoulders. FADE OUT.*) I prayed he'd visit me, or write, at least. He never did. Instead, his writer friends arrived much later that evening. Clearing the candle fumes, they came in twos.

WHITE CAPTION: Summer, 1951. FADE IN. *Wearing only a flowery nightgown, generic bra and corset, DI PRIMA sits on her mattress in dim candlelight. From the left speaker comes the (O.S.) sound of knocking, hoarse male shouts and stifled laughter. Holding her collar together with one hand, DI PRIMA runs to the door.*

DI PRIMA
(V.O.)

ALLEN and JACK were the ones who took my virginity.

Reluctantly, DI PRIMA opens the door. ALLEN GINSBERG and JACK KEROUAC stumble in.

I still remember the commotion in my bedroom. ALLEN's skull and belly gleamed in amber candlelight. JACK grinned handsomely as he lifted my dress to inspect my cherry.

MEDIUM SHOT *of KEROUAC ripping away a frozen DI PRIMA's dress. CLOSE-UP MONTAGE of brutal trespasses. Hands slip beneath the corset band. Knuckles arch. Tongues lick shadowy hollows and openings.*

They said they were going to fuck me, so I nervously undressed. Throughout that midnight orgy, I did everything I could to please them.

CLOSE-UP *of DI PRIMA's tear-stained face sandwiched between JACK's distracted grimace (FRONT) and ALLEN's leer (BACK).*

In return, they taught me lessons about life. But since I'd come of age as a fifties chick, their most important rule pertained to sex.

CUT TO *shot of KEROUAC using a teacher's pointer to jab*

at a spread-eagled, bound DI PRIMA as GINSBERG displays various typewriters and syringes. The two men ramble unintelligibly in the bg.

No matter how fat, stupid, or self-obsessed he is, the bohemian chick must always fuck her guest, JACK said. If you don't fuck your guest, that means you're just hung up.

CLOSE-UP *of DI PRIMA's eye, duct-taped open: trembling and wide.*

Since fucking everyone was cool according to JACK, and since those two guys were the first friends I ever had, I believed them. I couldn't very well go along with my parents, right? I didn't realize till later that JACK and ALLEN had *lied...*

FADE OUT *like a pause at the end of a stanza.*

The incident left me mute, but that didn't matter. I was on the inside. I was a beat chick. I knew the words.

(WHITE CAPTION: 1955.)
FADE IN *on* ORIGINAL SHOT *of DI PRIMA and IVAN.*

DI PRIMA
(V.O.)
It's hard to believe the orgy happened here.

CUT TO *IVAN, with the edges of DI PRIMA's legs and hands within the frame.*

IVAN
(Lazily rolling his R's) Vass gut, eh? Vassn't it gut, leetle Möte? Vassn't my vish fulfillment epizode gut for-r-r you-too?

CLOSE-UP. DI PRIMA, *almost expressionless but for a slight forced smile. She wants to speak but can only manage a few provocative grunts.*

DI PRIMA
Uh...Uh...

IVAN
(Sprechstimme) How I *luff* my *lee*-tle *feef*-ties *möte!* Der-r-r *mötes*, dey give der *pest ploh* jobs...

DI PRIMA
(V.O.)

I'd serviced him three times already, as I had so many other pigs. It was all they ever wanted anyway. So I couldn't tell him it sucked to suck him off. Let IVAN have all the pleasure for now, I thought. My turn would come later, when it was time for his *dissection.*

TRACK *IVAN's head turning widely, jaw relaxed, eyes clouded.*

DI PRIMA
(V.O.)

How I despised him—for his naive self-interest...

DI PRIMA'S POV *of IVAN's rib-cage stretched by fun-house mirror.*

...his gangly, greenish body...

INSERT *of undersea eels sliding across one another.* DISSOLVE *to* CLOSE-UP *of IVAN's lips.*

...his insufferable smile, his plumber's kiss...

REVERSE POV. FULL VIEW *of DI PRIMA nodding and grinning hollowly, her shoulders hunched, her knees folded, her legs drawn beneath her in the shape of an angular conch.*

DI PRIMA
Uh! Uh!

DI PRIMA
(V.O.)

All my disgust would be set down in a vehemence of gushing, logorrheic, Lawrentian rhetoric; in metanarrative so mercilessly sprawling it would destroy his confidence and subvert his memories of conquest. I looked forward to drowning his identity in a prose like theft, a prose of cons. But for now, the impulse to retaliate locked itself in my double-jointed replies. A working class rapist—how mindless, I thought. To IVAN, my grunts seemed counterfeit praise. All coined at his expense.

MEDIUM GROUP SHOT. *IVAN tosses DI PRIMA a work shirt and she pulls it over her head.*

DI PRIMA
(V.O.)
...just ignore the stench, I thought...
TRACK. *IVAN leaves bedroom through kitchen hallway.*
INSERT *of thirties cartoon urinal coughing.* CUT TO FULL
VIEW *of bedroom. IVAN whistles OFF-SCREEN until he walks*
INTO FRAME *with a plate of scrambled eggs.* CUT TO CLOSE-
UP *of DI PRIMA's nauseated grimace and protruding tongue.*

IVAN
Hey, Möte! Vant zum breakfazt?

DI PRIMA
(Disgusted) Uh! Uh!
*IVAN takes a bite, tries to kiss her with egg dripping from
his lips. She waves him off, leaves.*

IVAN
Möte go... to powder byootiful cheek, huh huh huh...
*DI PRIMA walks INTO FRAME in a beret and false goatee,
pulls out a Colt revolver with a Wilson Suppresser and shoots
IVAN. As he slides off the bed, too surprised even to feel
betrayed, she stands there, penumbral in hall-light, her shadow flooding the recessed floor at her feet with blackness.*

IVAN
(Moaning) Vot der-r-r-r fock!!...how can you come...
you ar-r-r-re friendly möte...

DI PRIMA
(V.O.)
(Facing the camera) Yeah, *I* was JACK KEROUAC's
fuckin' fifties mute, huh? I was definitely the slut queen no-
tell motel on *his* two-lane blacktop: a well-oiled wand-
warmer like all the other skanks. Yup, *all* us bitches got
fucked over in those days—knocked up, abandoned, raped
in our sleep by drunken poets, overlooked, cheated on, dis-
couraged (like Dorothy Wordsworth and Lady Montagu)

from writing our own novels—we *really* only existed to keep house, breed, or volunteer for the slit research of NEAL Fucking CASSADY. But all of that was about to change— permanently. When I finally found my own screwed-up voice, my music was murder to Charlie M. Parker's ears...

As IVAN moans, DI PRIMA pulls out a huge plastic book with a hollow center, opens it, lops off one of Ivan's hands, and throws it inside the book. Animated cartoon globules rise from his stump's spurting gore to the center of the frame, where they gather to form the ghastly red letters of the title:

DIANE DI PRIMA: MS. 55

dir. & wr. by Abel F. Cainan, low-key auteur

(Based on the unsubstantiated bragging
of DI PRIMA's cellmate, **SUSAN ATKINS**)

CLOSE-UP *of IVAN's face.* But—you are kill me? How can you come? You are female in feefties vorlt.

DI PRIMA
(V.O.)
Get over it. Centuries before the beats made a character flaw out of disciplined behavior, amazons conquered civilizations and women ruled. I've always known it intuitively, just as you grasp a woman's second-class status today. But I hadn't really understood the mindset of my homicidal ancestors until two years ago last Tuesday. The problem that solved it all was JACK, who had drenched my uterus in seed he'd promised to spill, leaving me with *his fetus*—a fetus for which JACK's delinquent head scoped zero responsibility. After nine months of indifferent recriminations, circumstances drove me to an act of murder: deserted by JACK, and too poor to enlist the aid of illegal doctors, I was forced to give *myself* a bloody abortion. It all seemed so painful at first (my hand shook violently, my scalpel felt cold

and biting, the hose leaked tiny body parts onto my gown) until I heard my sewage problem scream. I'd waited too long for the operation, and now JACK's...embryo...felt the pain acutely, a pain acutely expressed by his full-blown vocal cords. But when I murdered JACK's...child...I screamed more loudly than even it had screamed. That's when I first heard my own voice, the invention of a cribbed death, a murderer's emergence. Soon, I knew, my voice would swallow larger victims. An aborted life marked the end of my killing silence.

IVAN
(Suddenly waking from the pain) But...you kent do ziss ...If you are killer, dey vill say you are not real vooman...

DI PRIMA
(Aloud)
They won't say that—not ever. From now on, NEAL and JACK and ALLEN and the rest—that whole, interminable queue of braggarts and rapists—they'll know me as *MS. FIFTY-FIVE.* They'll christen me the snipercunt of cocksmith deadbeats, the one men ignore till she rips through their womb of come. So clear off the cobwebs, Faucet-Fist. After your testosterone dries to powdered vanilla Ovaltine, "they" will forget your manhood and remember my mien. *(Leans over and grabs IVAN by the hair)* I said, the name's di Prima, Mister...but *you* can call me *MS. FIFTY-FIVE.* Porn diarist and madam of murderous memoirs.

IVAN
(with his last gasp) Hey...you, lady möte, you...spoke to me... *(slumps forward and stiffens)*

DI PRIMA
(releasing IVAN's head) I always had it in me—or didn't you know? They say the last mute speaks when the loud man dies. (SLOW FADE.)

JULIA SOLIS

A DINNER FOR NIGHTMARES

m y friend diane used to invite me to dinner at her place on east fifth. she had nothing much to eat but at least she found these cool names for the things she served and i kind of admired that. she was real crazy about this dish called menstrual pudding that was just potatoes in tomato sauce and no spices or meat and it wasn't all that bad. i would go over there for lunch sometimes and supper, supper meaning a late dinner, and after a while she ran out of new potatoes for the pudding so we just added more water to the old ones and it got mushier and mushier. but diane still called it menstrual and that was really cool.

well i felt sorry for diane and these cats jack and brad who were staying with her and i decided to invite them to my place for a feast. it was a cold day in february, i remember and barren, but i thought if i invited enough people over to my room and we ate lots of food we would all stay warm. so i made up a menu that i copied onto little pieces of paper for everyone and i drew a border around the whole thing so it looked like a menu from a real expensive place. four seasons like.

first i served the blood clot soup. it was just hot tomato juice with some lumps of flour thrown in for the clot effect and no spices to distract from the tomato flavor. then i passed around the hydrocephalic slaw of pale bloated cabbage soaked in water, with osteoperosis breadsticks and candida septicemia cheese. to drink there was a choice of curried diarrhea milk or bladder infection nectar concocted from a few drops of fish sauce in water. i had gone all out and got some liver from a lithuanian butcher down by the hudson who was dirt cheap even if his organs were mostly overripe. here i got my cirrhosis roast. i was very proud of it, i had dotted the liver pieces with liquid bleach so they had bubbly pink and green spots that seeped right through the tough little fibers. it came with dysentery rice from mushy brown pebbles i picked up behind the stove, and creamed jaundice scraped out of a can of corn i found behind aunt tillie's diner. and of course i made a smoked hamartomatous periappendiceal salpingitic intravascular hemorrhaging streptococcal polypous metastatic hypertrophied purulent melanomalous pulmonary glomerulonephritic ulcerating hyperemia salad with a secret sauce. the desert, gonorrhea pastries, was the coup de grace. They were glazed with moist cat food whipped in a yellow sugar paste. the pastries smelled really real. or really cool as diane would say.

diane thought it was cute and that was what mattered because you need good friends to get through the winters in manhattan. And sure enough, soon after that the bad times began when there were bats and possums in the kitchen and little four-legged retards who tried to bite you when you squeezed by.

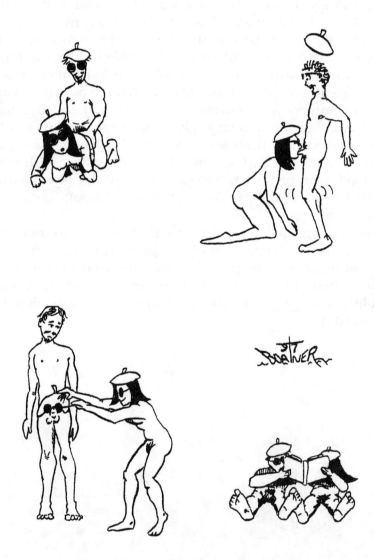

BONNY FINBERG

HOW I BECAME A BUDDHIST,
BY DIANE DI PRIMA

I t was around the time I was hanging around with Dave and Chuck and Linda. Linda always brought her dog, Joint, who had this giant dick. We were all on the mattress. Linda let out a moan from real deep in her throat, then a high pitched whine. Or was it Dave? He could make some way out noises. Though it could have been Chuck when Dave stuck his finger up his ass. Or did Linda stick it into Dave. Her and Chuck were trying to work out some jealousy thing. Oh wait, I remember now, it *was* Joint. Yes, it was Joint, it was definitely Joint. He had his dick in his mouth and got so carried away he bit it. Bit his own prick. But that's cool. It's better than sticking it in Linda. She had the clap. She got it from some guy she met at the counter at Longley's cafeteria. She really dug him too, she thought he dug her the same way. They saw each other for about three weeks. It was serious. They both dug the same things, dope, jazz, work shirts. It was intense. There were only about fifty of us in New York. Maybe a couple hundred in the whole country. We were so cool, we didn't even know each other existed, we all thought we were the only one. It was serious. So when one of us met another it was like some kind of crazy inter-galactic club. We sort of passed each other around and pretty soon it was like Gertrude Stein's *The Making of Americans*, and we were all of a repertoire of kinds. Even dogs were cool as long as they belonged to one of us. We all got the clap sooner or later.

We'd talk to strangers in Longley's sometimes, but that was just to enrich our inner lives for our art. We enriched our inner lives a lot. One time I went to visit Veronique, an old college roommate. She lived on a huge old Connecticut estate. The maid made kippers and ham and eggs, fresh squeezed orange juice and cafe au lait for breakfast. After breakfast, Veronique took me into the barn. We celebrated each other in great orgasms. She had an amazing ass. She gave me this groovy sweater from Saks. Then she told me she was a Republican. I stayed for dinner, Lobster Thermidor, then I told her what I thought about selling out and went back to New York.

That was right before I became a serious Buddhist. Dave and Chuck and Linda were over and we were sitting around naked on the dirty carpet we found rolled up in the street. We were smoking some hash, passing a Moroccan pipe that Allen Ginsberg gave to Janine, who gave it to Linda, who gave it to me. That's what Linda said anyway. But you couldn't always trust Linda because she'd say anything to smoke your drugs. She came over that night with the pipe and told us how she got it, saying she wished she had something good to inaugurate it with. She just so happened to have run into Dave on the street and he said he was on his way to my place. Dave was the biggest dealer below 14th St.

We were sitting on the rug arguing whether we should pull out the Tarot or the Ouija Board. Dave and Chuck both wanted the Tarot. They were like Fric and Frac, they both always wanted the same thing. It was cool during orgies but it was boring the rest of the time. Linda wanted the Ouija Board and I was saying it was just commercial goods, it was monopolized by Parker Brothers, part of a conspiracy to exploit the working man, a consumerist hype we were all being fed by advertising, by corporate interests, which controlled advertising and ultimately the Military-Industrial complex, who didn't even give credence to Ouija Boards but used the bread of the superstitious working class to feed the monstrous mouth of the Corporate-Military Machine. If we were going to do the Ouija Board, then we would have to make our own. We were not part of the superstitious working class. We didn't even work. So we passed around some paper and wrote a poem about it. The rule was the pipe and the paper had to land at the same time, so it took us a couple of hours. We were artists. Serious. Then we used the paper with the poem on it as the Ouija Board. We shaped this six inch diameter piece of hash into the puck. It was like psychic Knock Hockey, man. Instead of YES or NO answers we'd get the drift from the line the puck landed on. Dave's turn came. He asked the Ouija about which way he was going. He got the line "You think you're cool man, cause you put your big corporate dick into my virgin ass." We all knew what this meant. So him and Chuck went over to the mattress on the floor, cleared the stack of Kierkegaards and Bakhunins onto the floor, and got married right there. Linda looked at me and we got up and joined in the wedding party.

After that it was Chuck's turn. He asked the Board if him and Dave were going to last. The hash landed on the line, "Who needs gravy when there ain't no meat?" So obviously, and we all knew it immediately, he took Dave out to the fire escape and gave him the most beautiful blow job, crying the whole time, saying this was his gift to 14th street, and for all the people living on rice and beans. It was Linda's turn. She sucked on the pipe and closed her eyes. Serious chick. She asked if she'd ever meet Paul Bowles in person. We tried to give this our communal energy. We expanded into a vast Sahara, each of us a grain of sand reflecting the power of the sun. It landed on the line "you are not my mother, you are not my father, you are just another sucking mouth to feed." Linda had a vision of Paul Bowles sucking her breast and Jane Bowles going down on her. She told us she wanted to enact it with me and Dave. We went into the kitchen and got some milk. I poured it on her breasts and Dave licked it off while I helped myself to her honey pot. Chuck just sat there, still crying. He said we were wasting the milk and should give it to the poor people on 14th Street.

My turn came. I refilled the pipe and lit it. I asked the board, "What can I do to live my life in a way that is true to my true self?" Then I took a long sensuous drag on the pipe, like I was blowing that pipe till it came. I never felt more serious in my life. I held my fingertips lightly over the hash patty. It moved to the top, slowly shifted over to the right, then shot down to the bottom of the paper where we'd signed our names. It landed on *dianne di prima.* We all freaked. Then we hugged and cried. My eyes were open, I like looking. Chuck stuck his finger in Linda's ass. She moaned. He looked surprised. Then he pulled it out quick and stuck it into Dave's ass. Dave turned around and put his tongue on Linda's belly, working his way down. He had his finger in my ass. Linda stuck her toe in my cunt while she sucked Dave's cock. I alternated between the pipe and Joint. It was then that I realized how we are all one.

I chose the path of the Bodhisatva, which was the path truest to my self. I am still walking that path, everyday, in my simple life in the country with my five children. And it's like I always say, the best reason for having babies is: "Get welfare, quit working, stay home, stay stoned, and fuck"... seriously.

TOM SAVAGE

BEAT EGOS GO BUMP
IN ENLIGHTENMENT'S SHADOW

W hat is the sound of one hand clapping? Try hitting
your thumb against the fingers of the same hand
in a quiet place. Classical (Theravada) Buddhism
is extraordinarily clear and precise. Its guiding principle is
equanimity. Its practice requires a balanced mind, not the
mental extremes and intensities trumpeted by the best Beat
poetry. Theravada also happens to be what the Buddha,
himself, taught. The Romantic mystification attached to Zen
and other forms of the later developed Mahayana Buddhism
(Greater Vehicle) by members of the Beat generation made
Sisyphean strugglers with meditation out of many from their
audience who finally broke the pattern only to fall through
the psychic Earth's floor. Many, many others merely gave up
after months or years of trying. These luckier ones at least
avoided crashing in any permanent or longterm way.

Is it any accident that the Beat "big egos" chose the
Greater Vehicle over the "Lesser Vehicle" (Theravada
Buddhism of Thailand, Burma, and Sri Lanka)? As for the
Bodhisattva Vow, strapped to Cadillac dharma, it allows
them significantly to postpone their full enlightenment until
almost all beings become enlightened. This is expected to
take millions of years. Meanwhile, the fruits of big egodom
remain to be enjoyed. It's no accident that the gesture
behind "one hand clapping" is also the movement we make

to denote "talk, talk, talk." Nevertheless, the simplicity and directness of the gesture say more about what Shakyamuni was about that the hundreds of spiritual hierarchies which developed long after him. Devas are Buddhist angels or demi-gods. How many devas or Bodhisattvas can you fit on the head of a pin? Does this require at least two pins?

Although it is undoubtedly true that Greater or Lesser Vehicle, all vehicles will eventually be towed away at owner's expense, the lesser bill remains the more attractive. Simplicity and directness would appear to be virtues.

Kerouac was the first major literary self-proclaimed spokesperson for Buddhadharma in America. He was also the first to mix insight with intoxication. He died of the latter. Shortly before he died, Kerouac turned up intoxicated and incoherent on the William Buckley television program. So while some of his "Mexico City Blues" are clearly not only great poems but also purvey many aspects of the dharma that can be conveyed through reading, their impact on the bearer of the news appears to have been superficial. Transcending the ego was not intended to mean destroying its container. At the very least, psychic centering and an increase in psychological health are usual qualities of genuine Buddhist teachers. "Mad wisdom" wasn't meant to imply you let yourself go to pot. Also in the realm of intoxication, it happens that marijuana and harder drugs were glorified by some Beatniks who also proffered version of the Buddhadharma. Many human beings destroyed braincells with one simultaneous to the pursuit of the other. Although human beings use only 3% of their brains in normal activity, meditation would seem to require more than that to be effective.

There is also the question of mantras (repeated words or phrases). These concentrate the mind. But any words repeated in this fashion will do that. There is a danger with mantras that meditation can degenerate into hypnosis or self-hypnosis. The Beats who didn't glorify/mystify Zen koans promoted a succession of mantras for years. This left many of their followers treading psychic water as they jumped from one mantra puddle to another without ever getting either a full swim or, if you like, reaching the other shore.

Now that the fashion for the Beatnik version of Buddhism has long passed and contact with genuine teachers has become possible, it remains for those with a genuine interest in meditative psychic healing to pursue it and they do. One of the genuine contributions to "Western" dharma was made by a Tibetan teacher, glorified by Ginsberg, named Chogyam Trungpa. He taught his students to be wary of "spiritual materialism," the need to search for something and cling to various psychic states along the way. But Krishnamurti, a spiritual teacher who resisted all doctrines and meditative methods while teaching people how to meditate, put it most succinctly. He said: "If you are searching for something, mustn't you already have experienced it? If not, how would you recognize it when it arrives?" Krishnamurti lived to a very happy old age. Trungpa died of drink in middle years.

Many Westerners who were once on any of various spiritual paths, wearied of the one or many they pursued, and returned to the material materialism their forefathers taught them to pursue. Now we have school children murdering each other and the total dominance of most people's minds by the need for the acquisition of money. To many, meditation is now little more than a "relaxation technique," like jogging or gymnastic exercise. The Beats can possibly be blamed, in part, for the fact that a tradition of two thousand years development in Asia, had a kind of cactus-like flowering with the wind blowing the wrong way. Those who found and stayed with genuine teachers may be bringing about a change in the weather. What does it all have to do with poetry? Some great poetry has been produced along the way by poets who became monks or devoted many years to study as well as practice. At least one of the Beats, Philip Whalen, apparently went the whole poetic way. There are also others in the younger generations. Theravade, the Volkswagen dharma, seems to have yet to create a group of poets, although isolated individuals have practiced it. It may even be that poetic practice and meditation, while they give one another energy and play, shy away from sending us any more poetic spokespersons for awhile lest the sound of that breathing, clapping hand get so loud that it becomes just another advertising traffic jam along the way. Still the essence of what produces poetry is one-pointed, concentrated attention, the birthplace of Buddhist practice, as well.

It remains only for me to say that I make no claims to be more enlightened than anyone else on the Path. Those who make such claims tend to be among the most ego-deluded. Ultimately, both Vehicles head for the same parking lot. Still, a lot of mistranslation has had to be discarded along the way.

NANCY KOAN

THE BEATEN PATH

The big tumble was not far away. In less than a year I would be evicted and searching for shelter in the East Village. But for a time, I was still nestled rather comfortably in the Upper West Side and only vaguely contemplating a job. My good neighbor up there Carl was the kind of guy who liked new toys. He'd play with them for a while and then toss them my way. In this case, the toy was a week-long pass to the Dalai Llama's Kalichakra Initiation at Madison Square Garden. I took it eagerly, though as only an occasionally Ju-Bu (Jewish Buddhist), had no idea what the whole thing meant. It didn't matter. I was looking forward to deep breathing and sitting under the gaze of the Compassionate One.

As spectacles go, this one was pretty hot. Lots of mustard yellow robing and pretty hanging things. And, of course, Richard Gere's Armani clad prostrating butt was memorable. But for the most part I slept. Not all the time, just mostly. First I would chant, then read, then stare at the semi-famous Buddhists in the crowd and then fall out. Perhaps it was the heat, but I was told not to be concerned. I was still "getting it" unconsciously. I was connecting. This seemed enough for me and at least I wasn't at home worrying.

It was after lunch on the 5th day that I saw HIM. The Bearded Beat Bu-Ju himself, Mr. Ginsberg was dashing in to catch the afternoon service. He had probably come from a private session with the Dalai as he seemed a bit more tran-

scendent than the rest of the throng. I stopped him and asked him
if he remembered my interviewing him at Abbie Hoffman's memorial party. He didn't but said he did. I then asked him if he'd like to
see the film I made on Abbie. He inquired whether he was in it and
I replied that I had to cut all extraneous footage, 'cepting the interview with Mr. Hoffman. He then looked me in the eyes and said quite
plainly that he was very busy and only interested in viewing and collecting footage about himself. I was so stunned at his honesty that I
had to remember to close my jaw and upon reopening said something like, "Thank you anyway." He then turned and streamed into
the Paramount for afternoon prayers.

I have tried to let go as we are taught to do by the Buddha. To
non-attach to Mr. Ginsberg's attachment to himself. Abbie's dead
and couldn't care less if Allen Ginsberg wanted to see the film, so
why should I? Is it possible that in following the Buddhist path Mr.
G. did have an ego death at one time, but was full of ego all over
again. Like losing weight and putting it back on. Or having your
moles removed and finding them grow back a year later. Perhaps
the ego simply gets reborn all the time — Born Again Ego. Like a
loyal erection, hard to keep down. Maybe it's inconceivable to experience ego death only once in a lifetime. Maybe it's simply a matter
of constant rebirth and redeath and one must check oneself every
few years. Sort of like looking for ticks after a good, long stroll in
the woods. Smash the monster.

Whatever. I still a had a nice time that week and even dragged
myself to the sunrise service in Central Park. There was so much
yellow in the trees that I wouldn't have noticed Allen's ego anyway.
Just peaceful drumming to the Buddhist beat.

SAMUEL R. DELANY

BEATITUDES

§ 1. In his essay "Sodom: A Circuit Walk," Paul Hallam writes of a Gay Sunshine interview with Allen Ginsberg in which he "established, as a kind of Apostolic succession, his own homosexual descent from Whitman, by pointing out that he (Ginsberg) slept with Neal Cassady, who slept with Gavin Arthur, who slept with Edward Carpenter, who slept with Walt Whitman himself." Ginsberg added that this was "an interesting sort of thing to have as part of the mythology."

Well, back in the 'sixties I slept a couple of times with Chuck Bergman, then a very good looking, thirty-five year old Lower East Side landlord, who from time to time was sleeping with Ginsberg...

Chuck had a charming Puerto Rican girlfriend on the side, but when he was in bed with me, all he talked about was screwing Ginsberg, who, at the time, was living in one of Chuck's apartments. Apparently the apartment was subject to a lot of wear and tear, and Chuck was worried about his property, even though he was vastly honored by Ginsberg's presence—and quite happy to fall in bed with him. Chuck's constant talk of Ginsberg finally got kind of unnerving. I wonder if, at the time, I'd have felt differently had I known Carpenter and Whitman were in the picture.

§2. At the late-lamented Endicott Book Shop in 1985, William Gass gave a reading from Habitations of the Word. William Gaddis came that evening. At one point a photographer who'd done some pictures of me the year before got a shot of all three of us, looking practically as if we knew each other. With the reading proper about to begin, I was in my seat in the fourth row when I looked up to see Ginsberg, squeezing between the files of chairs. I was just about to move back, when he stepped squarely and heavily on my left foot—inadvertently, of course—and continued on to a chair further down.

Somehow that didn't seem the moment to run after him and mention that, twenty years before, we'd had a mutual bedmate.

§3. For the next half dozen years I was able to say that was my only face to face encounter with Allen (this heavy-footed recomplication in our intimacy, I figured, allowed me to call him by his first name; everyone else did), though actually he'd been looking over my head.

That changed in February '92, when I went down to Pennsylvania to participate in a gathering for the Associated Writing Programs. The '92 AWP Conference was honoring Ginsberg. I was part of a four-person panel on Gay Writing. At the reception upstairs in the Hershey Hotel, after the panel was over I was a bit surprised when, in his modest brown suit and tie, the scraggly bearded Professor Ginsberg came over to me and, quite out of the blue, said: "Hello, Delany. How've you been?" at which point for me he became Ginsberg again.

"Fine," I said—and put my left foot quickly behind my right. "And you?"

We launched into a chat about the Cherry Valley Farm and the Naropa Institute, that he ran with Anne Waldman. Finally he reached into his canvas shoulder bag and handed me a flier for a series of readings he and Gwendolyn Brooks had organized of (mostly) black poets.

It was an impressive list. He certainly got points from me for it. Shortly someone called him to the front of the room where, with Ed Sanders and Tuli Kupferberg, the Fugs had reconvened for the event, and Ginsberg led the whole room in singing lustily along to some Blake Song of Innocence.

To this day I don't know who told him what my name was. The next and last time I saw him?

One warmish winter day in '94 or '95, when, a bit after three, I was leaving my publisher's office on Second Avenue just up from 43rd Street, I turned from under the gold marquee and saw Ginsberg walking among the afternoon crowd, in the same direction I was, eight or nine feet away.

I thought about saying hello, but finally held my peace, glancing at him now and then. Soon, he was ahead of me. At 42nd Street he crossed over, to disappear among the people beyond the cars. Where might he have been going? Where might he have been coming from? Would anyone ever find the note I made of it in my journal, with date and time? I thought about the Poe Log and the Melville Log that chronicle those writers day by day, hour by hour. Might my note, a century hence, solve some scholarly mystery about the poet's doings that day?

Ginsberg's death last month means to me, more than anything, we are moving ahead into that century. We are leaving behind the old one which, for almost a hundred years, was the term for the indubitably new—even as, with the 19th, the 18th, the 17th, it takes its place in the past.

§4. An important psychological (if not sociological) transition for the young writer to undergo is the mental move from a world where literature is produced Out There, Somewhere, by mystical and mythical creatures who have no more reality than the characters in the books themselves, to a world where real men and women produce those texts that so enthrall us—men and women who, besides having the talent or genius for producing ones that delight, inform, or otherwise fascinate, and the ability to organize their lives so that these texts can find their way into print, are actual people, some Republicans, some Marxists, some with even stranger affiliations, living in actual houses, in specific neighborhoods. Some are even friends with one another. However Emily Dickenson effected such a mental transition in her second story bedroom overlooking Main Street in Amherst, or how Hart Crane got through it in his tower room in his grandmother's house at 1709, 115th Street in Cleveland, that transition alone is what allows the writer to harness her or his Begeisterung and write.

(The book that started the process off for me was Gertrude's Stein's endlessly wonderful Autobiography of Alice B. Toklas. I first read it in a Vintage paperback edition when, in 1959, I was seventeen.)

For writers my age, a few years older, or up to a decade younger, who were not a part of it, the Beat Generation and its poetic cohort, the San Francisco Renaissance (and, slightly less so, Black Mountain), was the first literary movement that we got to see, in the United States, up close.

What characterizes the Beats more than anything else was (paradoxically) not that they were beat, but that they were a generation—far more so than, say, the often chronicled "generation of 1914" or the target of Earnest Boyd's attack from twenties— "Aesthete: Model 1924" in the premiere edition of the American Mercury—on Gorham Munson, Hart Crane, Kenneth Burke, and Malcolm Cowley. These were a circle, yes. But a generation...?

It's worthwhile asking, then, why the Beats took on their special relation to those of us who were five, ten, fifteen years their juniors...

§5. When I was twelve, and confined to my room, I wrote angrily in a green leatherette diary with a brass clip lock: "When you grow up, it's important to let your children curse around you!" My father, profligate with his "goddams" and occasional "shits," had sent me there because, in front of my mother, I'd let slip a "damn." His unfairness burned through my whole body.

What, in another five years, the Beats came to represent for us (yes, at seventeen—when, on one weekend, the student demonstrations against desegregation flared at Little Rock, the news of Sputnik's orbiting the earth broke across the world, and in that Saturday's New York Times the highly sympathetic review of Kerouac's On the Road appeared that launched it on its career as the novel that would end the 'fifties and usher in the 'sixties) were the good, the permissive, the ideally fair fathers, who said you could smoke dope, wear your old clothes, let your hair grow, and cuss as much as you wanted.

Given that role, however, how could these free literary men and women, who grabbed our awareness by allowing the word to articulate any and every obscenity we kids could even consider (years after Howl was dragged into the courts in 1956, I remember arguing with a dismissive adult: "But don't you realize that was the first time a poem had been tried for obscenity since the fucking Flowers of Evil—and the Saturday Review of Literature never even mentioned it?"), possibly survive the transition—not of their growing up (the Beat-and-associated who lived did that remarkably well), but of ours?

§6. I met my *first* Beat poet in that selfsame seventeenth year—Diane DiPrima. (At the time, of course, I didn't know she was beat. She probably didn't either.) I'd been told lots about her, that she was incredibly intelligent, that she was a physics major who'd switched to literature, that she was great friends with dancer Freddy Herko, that she had an extraordinary child named Genie. When, one evening, she came upstairs from the printing shop where, with Le Roi Jones, she was putting together Unmuzzled Ox to drop in and sit in the front row (to the left) for the play and poetry reading I was directing and taking part in up at the Coffee Gallery, she was distant, a bit gawky, certainly not very approachable—although, during the wine and soda afterwards, I tried to be friendly.

She left quickly.

I doubt she was particularly impressed with the (most generous thing I can call it) neo-classical tone of the evening.

And she never knew that night she was speaking with a young man who had bought her first book at the Eighth Street Bookshop and knew poems in it by heart:

> Monos they say
> could never have
> a lover.
>
> They say men turned
> to earth who touched
> his flesh.
>
> They say
> he never
> wept.

from "The Life and Times of Monos." And, from the title poem:

> This kind of bird flies backwards,
> and this light breaks
> where no such shines.

Yeah, they were kind of Stephen Crane-y. Di Prima excluded those early efforts from her collected poems. But they'd meant a great deal to me—had even made me weep for dry-eyed Monos.

§7. The Beats' two New York City stamping grounds, the West End Bar across from Columbia University and the Cedar Street (on Eighth Street, just West of University Place), were the two bars in the City where I could get served beer regularly before I was eighteen. But my hours and the late hours of those writers and artists who circulated around the Beat movement never overlapped enough for me to meet any of them—though, before I was twenty I went once to the Cedar specifically because a friend of mine had gotten into a conversation there with Beckett the previous night, and I wanted to meet him.

He wasn't there, though—like Estragon, like Vladamir— I waited...

My distant "relationship" with Ginsberg, in its excessive

spottiness, among the vast lacunae waiting for imaginative in-filling, was pretty much characteristic of my relationship with the rest of the Beats and those associated with them. But the encounter with the writer is always fundamentally a mythical occurrence. And there certainly was no more mythical group of American writers in the central forty years —say 1940 to 1980—of this century. I mean: Sexton, Plath, and Starbuck hanging out after the workshop with Lowell, talking about suicide...? Jay McInerny having a drink with Raymond Carver when the creative writing class let out at Iowa...? No, I don't think so.

§8. A week before I took off for Europe in 1965 I got picked up by a painter named William McNeill, who, in the first twenty minutes I knew him, dropped what seemed to me, at least at the time, a hundred names of Beat and peripheral-Beat writers: Gary Snyder, Joanne Kyger, Helen Adam, Robert Duncan, Jack Spicer, Ferlinghetti, Michael McClure, Bob Kaufman...which is to say, the friends he was so anxious to let me know he had were writers and poets I had encountered in the Evergreen Review, including that famous 1957 Issue 2, the "San Francisco Scene," in which, eight years before, I'd first read Howl.

Four days in Luxemberg, two weeks in Paris, two weeks in Venice (now those were a couple of weeks to write about), and finally, by ferry, from Brindisi to Athens. After a handful of days in that city, we were two months on the islands, first on isolate Melos, then on more populous (but still, in the winter of '65/'66, fairly calm) Mykonos, and finally back in Athens by the second or third week of January.

A rough and vivid memory: sitting on the roof-patio of a small stone house in the picturesque neighborhood that, above the Plaka, clung to the back face of the Acropolis, like a displaced island village, with my friend DeLys, a delicate, golden-haired woman from New Orleans. (The stone houses were first built, ran the city's lore, by earthquake refugees from Anaphi island, so that the neighborhood was known as Anaphiotika: Little Anaphi.) While we sat, drinking Greek tea, someone down in the street shouted, "Hey—anybody home! Hey?" We looked over the edge.

Carrying some kind of dufflebag, a scruffy black-haired fellow in his thirties was doing the shouting. "Hey—it's Gregory. We're gonna crash here! Joyce said it was okay! Come on—let us in!"

Beside him stood a rangy blond guy, thumbs beneath wide drab backpack straps, watching while the other shouted: "Open the fuckin' door, will you? Let us in!"

DeLys called: "... who are you? What do you want?"

"Come on—it's Gregory! You gonna let us in or not? We're tired. Let us in, now—"

"I'm sorry. I don't know you... I think you must have the wrong place!"

"This is the place," the black-haired man declared. "Come on and let us the fuck in, now—I don't have time for this—"

At which point the blond one said, "Hey, come on—man! Fuck the bitch! We got those other places to try. Let's get goin'! Will you—?" He tugged the other by the arm. They turned—

—and loped off!

"Who in the world—" DeLys turned from the rail—"did they think they were?" She sat back down.

Though I'd only seen his picture on the back of his New Directions volumes (all of which I owned), I'd recognized him immediately: "That was Gregory Corso...!" I told her. (I had no idea who his companion was.) "I'm sure the Joyce he was talking about was your friend Joyce Johnson—the one whose book of poems you showed me...?"

At one time Johnson had rented the same house, I'd gathered, before DeLys had taken it over.

"Well," declared DeLys huffily, "I never met him before." Grape leaves on the trellis whispered; her yolk-pale hair lifted in the afternoon's first breeze. "He didn't sound like anyone I'd want staying with me!"

In the early sixties, Athens' itinerant winter internationals were just not that numerous. That same night I was at a party, somewhere nearer Colonaiki, where Gregory made a near-equally loud entrance, this time hanging all over the shoulders of an English red-head with whom he was now staying. Loud, opinionated, and probably stoned, he didn't remain long—and left to a buzz.

"That man," DeLys said to me, "is just awful! What is his problem?"

"Well," I told her, "he's one of the two most famous poets in the United States, right now. And of the two—" the other, was of course, Ginsberg—"I think he's the more talented. That can't be a very easy job."

"Well, I'm glad I didn't let him in my house!"

Since I was now staying on DeLys's living room daybed, I was glad she hadn't, too.

I had three more encounters with Corso—two in Athens, one in New York.

A few days later, at an iron table in the yard of a kafe-neon at the bottom of Mnisicleos Street, across from Babba Stavros's restaurant on the edge of the Agora of Diogenes (the Tyrant; not the Philosopher), conversation between half a dozen people interwove and tangled beneath the leaf-and-sun scumble through some leaning tree, when Gregory joined us—he knew someone in the group. That day he wasn't particularly loud or unpleasant: he was talking to another man there about a translation he was going to do of Euripides Bachantes. Somehow I got into the conversation with some comments about a production I had heard of but not seen in which Dionysus had been played by an nude actor. The man to whom Gregory was expostulating was unimpressed: "I can't see why anyone would want to do *that!*" But Gregory—possibly just to be eristic—thought it was a cool idea. Others at the table were leaving. Finally, the man said to Gregory: "Well—I'll see you for lunch at my place, then—tomorrow?"

With an explosion of enthusiasm, Gregory turned in his chair to drop a hand on my shoulder: "Can we bring this guy along? He's sounds pretty interesting!"

The man smiled at me: "Certainly—if you'd like." And to me: "That is, if you'd like to come...?"

I blurted, "I'd love to!" (I was twenty-three.)

He offered to write down his particulars in my notebook:

Alan Ansen, followed by a Colonaiki address. He left, and a moment later, Gregory was up: "Come on..."

—and I spent the next two hours, as I remember, running all over Athens with, or just behind, Gregory. Where we went or what he was doing, I no longer remember. But it was all very important at the time. In the course of it we had a lot of beer at various cafes, and there was much agonizing —from Gregory—about his up-coming Bachantes translation/adaptation.("This is a classic, see? You can't just fuck around!") I felt wonderfully privileged.

By the time, alone, I wandered back through the National Gardens and up through the Plaka to DeLys's in Anaphiotika, I was also pretty drunk.

But the next day I made it to Ansen's.

The apartment was clean, cool, and off-white. Signed Cocteau drawings hung on the walls; I couldn't have been more impressed by Picassos. Gregory was already there— he was actually cooking lunch for us! It was to be a kind of casserole that he'd volunteered to make in the well appointed little kitchen in a large, blackened Dutch oven! We sat around over glasses of white wine, with Gregory darting to the stove now and then.

Ansen asked me what I did, and I told him I was writing a novel about Jean Harlow, Christ, Orpheus, and Billy the Kid.

Leaning forward on the white table, Gregory said: "Jean Harlow? Christ, Orpheus, Billy the Kid, those three I can understand. But what's a young spade writer like you doing all caught up with the Great White Bitch?" Then he frowned for a moment, sitting back. "Of course, I guess it's pretty obvious."

Then lunch came to the table.

The little red peppers that Gregory had used in the casserole turned out to have been unbelievably hot. After one bite, Gregory put his fork down and declared: "Oh, Man —I fucked up! Come on. You guys don't have to eat this shit...!"

Actually, though, it was pretty good.

I was hungry, and I've always liked hot food. Ansen and

I both persevered through a helping each.

I said thank you and left—and did not see Gregory against for half a dozen years.

§9. It was back in New York on the Lower East Side. It was summer; it was hot; it was muggy. Walking down Ninth or Eleventh or one of those street over on A, B, or C, I saw a man, in a dirty white shirt and ratty black jeans, sitting in a doorway, with not a lot of teeth. Three steps later, I realized it was Gregory.

I went up and said hello.

He was pretty out of it. Did he remember me? Or the over peppery casserole at Ansen's? Had he ever seen the quote from our conversation that afternoon that had appeared, by now, as a chapter epigraph in my novel, published a few years before by Ace Books? He answered no to all of them.

"Are you going to be sitting here for a while...?" I asked tentatively,

"Man, I'm not going anywhere...!" he said thickly.

"I'll bring you a copy of the book!" I said. "I only live a few blocks from here." And I ran off to get him one. Though I was back in seven minutes by the clock, of course he was gone.

§10. Is there any point in telling the story of how, at a party on Henry Street, artist and set designer Robert LeVigne—his picture is in a dozen photograph books of the beat writers of San Francisco—chased me around a table with sex on the brain? Fortunately guests arrived before he could catch me.

My hopelessly unrequited infatuation, in '69, with Ronnie Primak, the poet who worked as a bartender in North Beach, where, in the slant light through dim shutters, we'd sit and jaw with Richard Brautigan at the bar...

Or how, at a drink-soaked dinner at Robert Berg's in San Francisco, I ended up falling into bed with poet John Ryan —I'm sure increasing my "Apostolic succession" by dozens on dozens of dozens!

Rather than anything sexual, however, my strongest memory of San Francisco—six or more years after the death of Jack Spicer—is a reading Anne Waldman gave in that city, in that summer, where someone threw a beer can at the podium while she was in the midst of a poem, somebody else got sick in the audience and someone else, drunk, staggered loudly in, then out. Anne's reading was electric, extravagant, and wonderful as always. ("My God," she said, when she came off, "when that beer can came at me, I was scared to death!") As we were leaving, poet Jack Thibeau said to me: "This is the *dregs* of a scene! It's not even the end of one. it's the morning-after dregs...!"

§11. Do such successions as Ginsberg spoke of to the Gay Sunshine people ever actually end?

But if we allow them into our genealogies, we must be free to criticize them.

It was sometime in the eighties that I went to a film at MOMA devoted to Kerouac and reminiscences of him by his friends, John Cleland Holmes, Burroughs, Ginsberg, Johnson, the Charterses. I don't remember the title, but I believe poet Lewis McAdams had been involved with its making.

It was something of a revelation.

The surprise was not that Kerouac had been—like Ginsberg, like Corso—devoted and fanatical about literature and poetry as he was. (People who are not fanatical about literature do not produce works that strike people as new and energetic: rather they produce works just like everybody else's. Knowing what literature is is the only way one can change and develop it; these writers had actually done that.) What surprised me was that, other than this fanatical devotion, Kerouac was such an extraordinarily ordinary man.

What he wanted to do—other than read and write—was to drink and fuck women. As far as I can gather, that was his only ambition for either the world or himself.

And this was the man that the circle—the generation around him—idolized.

To include drinking and fucking among one's ambitions is more than understandable. They are among mine. But to have no others seems limited, if not outright retrograde.

Because he was a charismatically handsome man, I can understand how more-or-less heterosexual Kerouac might have formed a focus for the particular group of extraordinarily intelligent gay men who clustered around him—for a season, perhaps. An extraordinary writer? I'll grant it. That he wanted to learn from them all about the literary—certainly, that must have been flattering to them. But from all one hears, the only thing life held for him besides that was going into a bar and cutting out the woman he could get drunkest fastest and home to his place or hers—unless some guy, after his bod, managed to get him drunker faster.

Good food? Companionship? Theater? Dance? Teaching the young? Helping the poor? The oppressed? Changing the world—making it a better place either for art or for life (or even for drinking and screwing), or even showing it the truth about itself...? Power, evil, making money—even those, as ambitions, at least teach us about ambition and its range of successes and failures. But the cosmic yearning that informs so much of Kerouac's prose turns out, in the life, in the long run, to be only the desire for mom to take care of him—and the drunken search for that night's mom substitute: no, he was a monumentally ordinary and unambitious man—which is to say, he was an extraordinarily wounded one, whose only concern (perhaps it was the only concern he could support) was with what, for most of us, are acts of self-healing. Yes, like all human actions not overtly unkind, they have a beauty in themselves. Still, once healed, to what end this body, this mind...? To what greater task...? I'm sorry. I don't get it.

These men's (and, indeed, women's) idolization of Kerouac the man—not the writer—strikes me as the greatest irony, if not the tragedy, in that generation's story.

— New York
June 1997

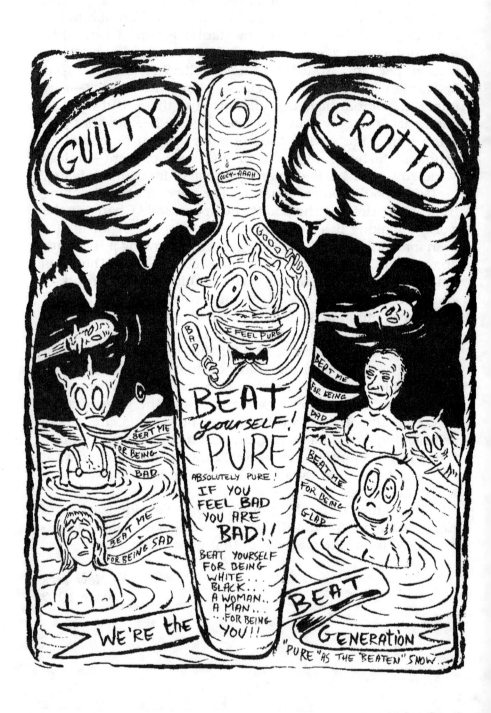

CHRISTIAN X. HUNTER

LETTER TO AMIRI

Dear Amiri,
Doubtless you know that the revolution
will not be television
But by now I would have thought
you'd have caught on that it will not be
Po-Lite
It will, you tell us, not be won
by standing around bitching about the
opposition
conversely
It will not be won by curmudgeonly
attacks on supportive fellow revolutionaries
It will not be
an intellectual patriarchy
It will not be won by
standing at the pulpit saying
Nhya ya, nhya ya, my revolution is
better than your revolution
In fact, the revolution will not be *won*
in the lump-sum, final goal, sense of the word
Revolution is
enduring
a process
Revolution
is Evolution
speeded up momentarily

by the voices of dissent
usually
not
the polite kind
Revolution is a response
by the responsible
and not the empty hand of cleverly rehashed rhetoric
Revolution is people
and how they relate to people
It is not a concept
It is A Love Cohesion
and would necessarily be empty and unfinished without the
elements of tolerance, forbearance and justice
for those who are unknown
or unknowable
those who we perceive as alien
and those whose agenda
moves along a parallel track
instead of settling for being a caboose
on the Baraka Express
The Revolution will not be aided
by those who criticize
what they don't understand
The Revolution will not be aided
by hypocritical men who sleep
with other men and then say
"Oh, I was drunk."
The Revolution will not be aided
by those who vainly bury the living
or abandon loved ones like they were obsolete ideologies
The Revolution may, at times, be temporarily
sidetracked
by those who insist on using
outmoded tools like
guns
though the opposition
will always have bigger and better guns

The Revolution will be momentarily
halted from time to time
while we all stop to see which
bad boy having reached political puberty
has wrestled his way
on to the national soapbox
to vent the finely tuned
and sharply focused fire
that quickly cools and dissipates in
the opposition's bottomless well of disdain,
and contempt for self-important
self-aggrandizing
icons of dissent
The Revolution *will* be aided by
those like Malcolm
who with grace and courage
put down the blindfold of rage
long enough to see that
the revolution is not
for the narrow minded
and the self-righteous
long enough to see that healing
and wholeness will never
arrive in the hands
of those who
unwittingly mirror the
opposition by practicing
the politics of exclusion.

TSAURAH LITZKY

REFLECTIONS ON BEAT SEXISM

Oh, oh, oh those beat men, those heroes of *On The Road*, those sweet sperm-spewing Apache dancers, darting from woman to woman like besotted fish trying to escape their karmic pond; the stick shifty, Howdy Doody truth and beauty of '50s America, that poor Neal Cassady squawking around like a rooster about to lose his neck, treating women like they were interchangeable Chinese launderettes, a cheap place to steam out the daily blue work shirt and get the greasy psyche clean.

I just re-read *On The Road* after 30 years. The mind bending-extending poetry-prose was even better but why didn't I notice when I first read it that the women were treated like inflatable rubber sex dolls? Maybe I wanted to be on the road with Sal and Dean, stopping to visit Old Bull Lee or Carlo Marx, maybe marriage, 2.3 legally conceived babies (the tuna and cheese casserole life was already anathema to me).

At 15, I knew I would never be an ideal woman, never look like Natalie Wood in *Splendor in the Grass*, never be placid and docile like Jane Wyatt on *Father Knows Best*. The role of a gone, Zen, wanton slut was infinitely more attractive, the idea that women were entitled to direct and participate in their own lives was still so revolutionary I didn't realize the itch between my legs was not lust for Neal Cassady but the first pangs of a collective yeast infection that would spread to so many women that we could only cure ourselves by birthing a new woman's consciousness.

On page 168 of *On The Road*, Dean and Sal are talking about the wife of a man named Walter. She was "the sweetest women in the world, she smiled and smiled." Dean says, "now you see, man, that's a real woman for you, never a harsh word, never a complaint, her old man comes in any hour of the night with anybody and has talks in the kitchen and drinks beer and leaves." This is not a woman Dean is describing, it is a catatonic doormat, but can I debunk or revile Kerouac for sexist writing when he was honestly expressing the passion and constipation of his time, and isn't that what a writer is supposed to do? His ear was clear as crystal. *On The Road* mirrors the Mamie Eisenhower meets Zorro character of '50s American romance. How could Jack Kerouac not abandon lovely Mexican Terry in a migrant worker's shack, it would have been inconsistent with his muse, his life, his times, not to do so. No wonder the women of *On The Road* were gullible and lonely and no wonder so many of them were waitresses.

What is scary is the influence of *On The Road* on a whole generation of American men, my generation. When my boyfriend returned from Mexico in 1960 where he had gone to score grass, he boasted of his adventures in the brothels of Tijuana and he had some suggestions about how I could perform a better blow job. I listened without a peep, even though I was crying.

Re-reading *On The Road* was as empowering as the thought of a hysterectomy. Without the mass marketing of the birth control pill in the '60s, would women have gone on to write manuals on how to perform cunnilingus, write books of poetry that would win Pulitzer prizes, become rocket scientists, corporate raiders, or motorcycle mechanics, who knows?

I am happy that men are still men and that women are no longer marshmallow fluff, at least not always, but despite the advances of feminism, women keep running back to men who beat and abuse them. Kerouac died estranged from his only daughter, Thelma and Louise had to drive off a cliff to preserve their freedom. Do women and men trust each other more now than they did 40 years ago? Maybe as we approach the millennium we will lay down our fears and find a higher road, maybe not.

DENISE DUHAMEL

BEATNIK BARBIE

Talk about failure.
Barbie couldn't snap.
Her fingers, Venetian blinds
that refused to spread. Her thumb,
stiff and apart. No hep cat,
she had voluminous hair, too easily
flattened under stylish berets.
A face that could express so little
of the anger of her times. When she tried
to go barefoot, the balls of her tip-toed feet
grew tired and calloused. She liked the fringe,
the tie dye, and psychedelic posters.
Her friend Andy Warhol even did her portrait.
But she hadn't the veins for heroin,
the lungs for pot, the rhythm for jazz.
She preferred glamour to Ginsberg,
fashion to Ferlinghetti,
winsome beauty to William Burroughs.

"TWO BEATNIKS"

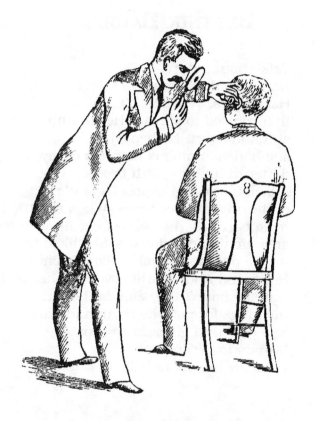

or "GUYS, POSING"

JUDY NYLON

MANNERS FOR THE NEW MILLENNIUM

"An anarchist with manners is called a leader."
Tommy Nylon 1954
Harvard Square

T he everlasting legacy of Beat is the black turtleneck, most recently spotted among the Algerian intellectuals, a red flag to the fundamentalist mullahs. It's the mute symbol of the questioning mind. It fulfills the basic tenet of what constitutes durability in the way Beat writing never did; it's universal and, as an emblem, vague. It transcends any agenda the producer may have had, gender, race, language, religion and so forth. Who really cares whether Juliette Greco, Ginsberg or Maynard G. Krebbs had one first? Even fashion can't really lay a hand on it. Figuring a time for the turtleneck or figuring a time frame for Beat is silly. Like every other entry on the exquisite corpse of culture, by the time you saw it, the comet had passed. If the culture comet was your joyful, spontaneous act, the public wants to pay you ten or thirty years later if you'll do it again. By then it feels like an unbecoming party trick or at least it should.

So what's the question hovering around black turtlenecks? I don't know; maybe it's something like: Are you sure you can tell the difference between a problem and a paradox? A problem has a solution; a paradox, you learn to live with. Beats whined against living with paradoxes, but they didn't solve any problems.

Beats failed to realize that they were connecting to a shadow history that's always been there like the reflection in glass. Post-Newtonian science has upped the ante of common knowledge. We know that there's no such thing as security; nothing's solid, no matter how far down into the subatomic you go, it's all energy. There's no loss to lament. Light is the closest thing to essence in the spectrum of the senses and the Beat world was notorious for being an orgy of bad lighting. Beats confused bad lighting with truth. Truth is a cubist thing; the universe through an enormous fly's eye, certainly no more apparent under a naked hanging bulb or believable because it's up lit like a horror film threat. I suppose it's not surprising that their highs never made the transcendent leap to making everyday actions and objects into the reflections of un-see-able beauty. Philosophy and religion are not a separate category from house cleaning and mending. Personal grooming is a courtesy to others; there are better ways to suggest an introspective life than wearing ripped clothes and a grimace. But this was all there in the Buddhist texts they had. Who knows why they missed it; maybe because if you buy into the cult of the rugged individual, the loner denies the interrelated universe.

Now might be the time to learn worldwide codes of etiquette for the same reason that beats found out what was transgressive or taboo. Confrontation can be sophisticated. Free speech is not about getting the permission to scream the odd vulgar word in a public place, but about being able to concisely state an opinion, in faultless form, without having been suckered by propaganda. Your sexual experiences and petty grievances do not automatically become art in their revelation. Both Beat action and Beat verbs lacked subtlety. Etiquette, functioning as baby steps to ethics and lessening the load of what needs to be covered by laws, could be the way to override the radar of mob thought. Manners are not a censorship tool. In the new millennium, it's all broadcast, you need something to surface through the static. All media's got an off and on switch; no one reads all their mail, let alone everything else coming at them. You can't even count on those fifteen minutes that were a sixties promise. If you know better than to point an umbrella at anyone in Burma, which three fingers to eat with (and only to the first knuckle) at an Arabic feast, and can indicate no sexual agenda by kissing a hand without letting your lips touch it, then you just might be able to live with the paradox of freedom by having the longest leash. Beats, with a disdain of etiquette and a false notion of freedom, limited themselves to a very narrow range of experience with a narrow range of people; "on the road" was a gerbil wheel.

Neither poverty nor wealth makes you holy; it's a separate issue. This love cry in the affair with America was sung in a very limited voice ranging only from butch homosocial to loner macho and always in the key of male. They hit the wall rather than deal with the female principle.

So here we are in the Age of Technology. The computer nets have already increased the speed, volume and distance of communication, but lobbed off the inflection of voice, language of gesture and any communication that humans use above language. The real agenda of technology is not to free time and develop human-kind, it's to sell you the customized multiple, object or desire. It's an ideal moment to inject the female principle, whatever it is exactly, into the machine. Maybe it's an analog for compassion, intuition, or an intangible way to inform the broadcast. Before you start composing, writing, painting, or whatever you think is so damned important...dress like a samurai; assume yourself ready for life or electronic immortality. Start with your intimates or go out and stay out until you've performed several acts of kindness and consideration.

In *The Alexandria Quartet*, Durrell put a quote in the mouth of his Pursewarden character, "The object of writing is to grow a personality which in the end enables man to transcend art." It's also fifties speak, but it beats Beat.

LORRAINE SCHEIN

BASIC BLACK

In the East Village
The punks wear black
The rockers and mods before them wore black
The beats before them wore black
And the rabbis before them wore black.
Black
Is the color of abject conformity.

CAROL WIERZBICKI

BEATNIK CUISINE

W hy gazpacho? The Beats were under many ethnic influences when it came to food, long before nachos and pizza were household words. Kerouac liked Mexican food. As Marge Piercy said of her college beatnik friends, "We put ouzo on shrimp and capers in spaghetti." And Etta Burroughs, William's grandmother, made gazpacho. She got the recipe from her visit to Spain in 1896, which deeply influenced her palate. While she chopped, Etta recited a favorite limerick:

> A young Naval ensign named Bates
> Like to do the fandango on skates
> Til he fell on his cutlass
> Which rendered him nutless
> And practically useless on dates!

Etta used to poke the Burroughs childrens' hands with a fork if she found their table manners wanting — an eerie precursor to William's later lifestyle. Hew favorite saying was: "If you don't stay out of my kitchen, the cookies ain't gonna get baked."

CHRIS BRANDT

CRIMES OF THE BEATS! CRIMES OF THE BEATS! EXTRA! EXTRA! BEATNIKS REALLY CRIMINALS! READ ALL ABOUT IT! BONGO POETRY RETROACTIVELY DECLARED A CRIME!

P icture two high schoolers in 1959, dressed in black, conversing philosophically over coffee at the ice cream parlor across the park square from the high school and the closest thing in Colorado Springs to what we imagined a Paris cafe might be. Dave Case and me. Talking seriously, smoking, drinking the coffee as if it were spiked with some exotic bohemian liquor, absinthe maybe. If we looked and acted like beatniks, we'd know what it was all about. We'd become beatniks. And how we wished it! Our difference named, our intellectual superiority perhaps resented but anyway recognized, we would...what? Lead our benighted burg out of its backwardness into cosmopolitan culture? Get out ourselves, and get to a place of like-minded people? No, I think we thought if we became beats all our roiling adolescent *sturm und drang* would take shape and form itself into the art we knew we were destined to make. Great art, goes without saying. We had no idea where to begin or how to go forward. So we dressed in black, let our hair grow (between enforced cuttings), drank coffee at Barthel's, smoked cigarettes, were *bad*.

BEATS REFUSE TO RESPECT ELDERS, OBSERVE SOCIAL OR LITERARY NORMS!

Picture my father, severe European academic, incensed at my appearance — a touch ragged, trying to grow a beard, slackly defiant—"You look like some Beatnik!" Imagine my reaction, outwardly disdaining to show any at all, inwardly tumbling with joy that I look like a *beatnik*! I wanted to shout, "Really? Do I really? Are you sure?" But that would blow my cool. So I twisted my mouth in resigned exasperation — he could be such an asshole — and turned my eloquent back. An imitation of him, in desperate irony. He didn't get it. Nobody got it. That was part of being a teenage beatnik. Oh, please, let me be misunderstood.

BEATNIKS A BAD INFLUENCE ON YOUNG, SAY OLD. ENCOURAGE LOOSE LIVING, SEX, THOUGHT. MAY BE COMMIE PLOT.

We never saw a beatnik in Colorado Springs. We read about them in *Time*, we looked at North Beach pictures in *Life*, but we never knew what they were about. What we were about, under their banner, was getting the hell out of Colorado Springs, away from oppressive families, out to the place of rebellion and freedom. Or, since we had no idea where that was, maybe we were about pretending such brave revolt, without ever having to leave the safety of our familiar discontents. Because I remember the feeling when I did really leave, to come east to college — I was scared, and later I was genuinely homesick.

**BEAT CULTURE THREAT TO AMERICAN VALUES.
ALLIED WITH DRUG, JAZZ UNDERGROUND. "DIS-
TINCTLY UNAMERICAN" SAYS MAYOR.**

The only time I saw a real beatnik — not an ex-beatnik in a sport coat and tie but a beat in the time of beats — was in the early sixties, probably '63 or '64, when Corso, Ferlinghetti, and Ginsberg came to read at Princeton. It wasn't an official university function — such occasions as now celebrate the safe enshrinement of beat culture in the past. Then, such people were still outside the pale — the English Department had nothing to do with it, nor did any other official organ of university culture. The reading was held in a poorly ventilated room in the Engineering School, where the readers sat on cushions on the floor in the front and the audience sat on chairs. The day was stifling hot, the acoustics were terrible, the lighting was institutional fluorescents, and from anywhere behind the second row it was impossible to see the readers. I fell asleep.

**BEATS BEAT RETREAT.
MANY FORMER BOHEMIANS WEAR JACKETS
AND TIES IN ACADEMIA.
SURVIVING BEATS SELL HISTORY FOR MILLIONS.
BEAT IMAGE LICENSED TO GAP.**

NATIONAL ENQUIRER COVERS THE BEATNIKS

(A COLLECTION OF ARTICLES ABOUT THE BEATNIKS
THAT HAVE APPEARED IN THE *NATIONAL ENQUIRER*
SINCE 1970: COMPILED BY BART PLANTENGA)

1. "BEATNIK BABY IS MODEL FOR MOVIE MONSTERS"
(May 1991) By FERMAN BELITTLE

*Hollywood director David Cronenberg claims his monsters
for the movie* Naked Lunch *were modelled after the real life
"Elephant Man love-child" of shock-beatnik author William
Burroughs and wife Joan Vollman.*

I didn't want to believe it and DIDN'T, until I heard him —
or IT — actually speak from its leathery gills" Hollywood
director David Cronenberg admits, "in that famous pinched
Burroughs twang."

This horrifying human oddity was apparently conceived in a
Mexico "Heroin Hacienda" during a drug shooting binge in 1951.
The lizard-skinned "love child" named Jimbo has, until now,
been kept out of the public eye at the request of Burroughs.

Cronenberg claims he was introduced to Jimbo after a jilt-
ed adolescent Moroccan lover of Burroughs first approached
National Inquirer with information leading to his discovery on
a Tijuana mescal cactus farm, owned by Burroughs and
another beatnik, buddhist budget advisor, Gary Snyder.

Cronenberg claims he was "shocked" to see an actual
"breathing Elephant Man" who looked like the embodiment
of his very own special effects dreams.

"It was like standing face to snout with the very nightmare that's dogged me all these years I've been thinking of
making *Naked Lunch* into a film."

What does "Jimbo" look like? Well, Cronenberg says all photos he took during his encounter have all been destroyed "to protect the fragile sanity of this crazy science experiment gone bad in the womb. Just see the movie!" But... and Cronenberg relents, "He's got leathery gills, long carbuncle-covered piano-playing fingers, hair like Wayne Newton, webbed feet and lidless, unblinking eyes."

Cronenberg says he's in the process of suing the Just Say No Foundation, a Heritage Foundation anti-drug lobbying group, which persists in spreading "vicious rumors" that Cronenberg once proposed Jimbo be used as an example, "a freak result", of the horrors of drug addiction. "They are viciously wrong. I'm not in the business of promoting freak shows."

2. "REPORTER UNDER COVER OF BEATNIK BLUBBER" (July 1985) By CLIFF BRIDGES

Our intrepid reporter Cliff Bridges put on his quilted blubber jacket (developed by Hollywood special effects labs for movie stuntmen) to tail porn publisher Al Goldstein. Instead, the ever-enterprising egomaniac Goldstein befriended Bridges and invited him along for a peek into a day in the filth-littered life of Al Goldstein. (Third in a series of 8.)

One of my many highlights as Goldstein's "blubber brother" occurred when A.G., portly prince of porn, stood in one night at the St. Mark's Poetry Project FUNdament Festival for another famed A.G., Allen Ginsberg. Ginsberg is known as the High Beatnik Queen of Porcine Poetry around this notorious temple of cool, sexy sacrilege, located along the seamy and steamy streets of Greenwich Village where everything — except decency and modesty — is allowed.

Here "our" A.G. got to read his very "own" poem called "St. Sebastian You & Your Bastard Tight Mouth" before a ragged if adoring audience of 400 "Wannabeats" and "Has Been Hippies." This poem was ghost-penned, our A.G. was proud to point out, by one of his many scrivening ghost-writers (mostly drug-addict-hookers who are plied with promises of low-resolution VHS porn fame).

An especially memorable line reveals the perverse verse of A.G. that so easily passes for poetry here: "Gerard de

Nerval from the lamppost you hung in desperate Paris nite,
& I swung from your hardon & stirred all in sight with the
howl that furnished my bowels with light!"

After his well-received reading (rapid & expressive snapping of fingers STILL serves as applause in THIS Beatnik
Temple), "our" A.G. quickly retreated to the church's urinary
facilities at that point. He strode into a toilet stall and here
behind closed doors, poured forth his meager spigot oozings
into the gratified maw of a young post-Joe Dellasandro pla-
giarism, who truly believes he'll get to proofread the new
Allen Ginsberg Book, *New York, My Incontinent Lover,* by ser-
vicing the plumbing of this very *other* A.G.

3. "FILTH IS ART TO WANNABEATS" (May 1993)

*A recent survey of 1500 Self-declared "Wannabeats and
Has Been Hippies" by Professor Laimin Potts, Director of the
Center of Jazz Poetry at Milford Community College in Milford,
PA, reveals that these "post-beat posers" are beating more than
just their bongos. They are beating down the doors of Madison
Avenue while beating their own chests louder than any ever
thought possible while continuing their time-worn tradition of
sacrilegious "tweaking of norms." Prof. Potts describes these
"tweaking of norms" as a "jealous attack on the very happi-
ness us middle class Americans hold so dear." We at NQ hear
this as the mere drums of conformity or, in the words of Prof.
Potts, "the infantile attention getting akin to the child's need to
fling feces at his mom."*

Professor Potts posed 10 imaginary situations to our
sample of 1500, dredging up, among others, the demi-gods
of Beatdom, William Sewer Burroughs, penman of many
unreadable and obscene so-called novels, including the
recent immoral box office bomb "Naked Lunch":

If William Burroughs were to urinate in his BVD's:
• **62%** of our sample of Wannabeats claim they'd be able
to divine the future from reading the resultant urine stains
the way seers can read the future in tea leaves or the stars!
• **70%** say if these BVD's were hung in an art gallery
they'd have "no problem" calling it art!
• **47%** would consider any latent scent "pleasing" to the nose!

• **24%** would go further and declare the scent arousing!

• **28%** would have no qualms about receiving a dream pillow stuffed with the urine-stained BVD's of Burroughs!

• **52%** would pay upwards of $20 to witness the act of BVD despoilation and would have "no trouble calling it performance art!"

In response to another scenario posed by Professor Potts, these same "Wannabeats", to the tune of:

• **66%** would rather send the starving Somalians chapbooks of Beatnik poetry than boxes of Cheerios!

• **72%** would rather donate Jazz records than Spam. While an astounding

• **79%** would rather the USA send chewing gum than Bibles!

(The survey is a scientific sampling of 1500 "self-declared Wannabeats", mostly urban performers dressed in the latest "Beat chic" and living quite comfortably on the stylish edge of society. There is a 3% margin of error. Complete results available through this publication.)

4. "PUNKNIK CLAIMS BEATNIK SEX SHENANIGANS" (April 1990) By KATI BOWELL

First there was Mommie Dearest, then came the child abuse accusations of LaToya Jackson, Oprah Winfrey and Roseanne Barre. Now porn plagiarist Kathy Acker, darling of the punk rock writing scene, claims that she, NOT Joan Vollman, was the one William Burroughs shot in a small Mexican border "Heroin Hacienda".

Kathy Acker, with her "prison chic" shaven noggin and bifurcated primate penis earrings wants to be taken seriously as a writer — as well as a victim! She claims she was only 6 years old when she was drugged with "mescal, heroin and chocolate bars" by the Burroughs. Then they played out their notorious William Tell drama with Acker being the one balancing the glass on HER head.

"I was really kidnapped by them and was the victim of a cruel bait & switch child abuse scheme." Acker claims. "But I eventually learned to love them!"

Acker further claims that she was shot in place of Burroughs' wife, Vollman, so that this charade, this "manufactured death" could allow Vollman to pass for dead and withdraw from the beatnik lifestyle she had come to despise. (She now lives comfortably with her electrician husband in a suburb of Grand Rapids, MI).

"Yea, there was a shooting—of sorts—and a disappearance too, but there was no death." Acker says, "A gun was discharged and one woman was liberated while another was enslaved."

But upon further questioning Acker admitted that the head injury she received (she NEVER refers to it as a head injury, preferring the more poetic "acquisition of a 3rd eye") was not incurred with a loaded pistol at all! No. The crime (or "rite of passage") involved an infected fountain pen that had been dipped into a "viral inkwell & thrust at my frontal lobes."

She claims she was "repeatedly stabbed and jabbed" with the infected pen over the course of a year by the Burroughs' who sought her "subclavian artery and any other arteries that carry blood from heart to brain," using an old Mexican human anatomy text as their guide.

She wears her close-cropped locks to show off her forehead scar because she is resentful but, at the same time, thankful. "My scar, my third eye, gives me a kind of advantage, like a red badge of courage. It makes me less logical, less bound by convention. It made me the writer I am today and mirrors the post-mod decay of narrative and critical acumen that I pioneered."

"I suffer minor brain damage. I have bouts of Tourette Syndrome. I'll suddenly break out into cursing and sexual invective right in the middle of a beautiful description of a French meadow but I've managed to make my affliction seem like a writing style." Whether it be hairstyle or writing style, Acker vows she will continue to live on the razor's edge of social convention.

5. "COMPUTER VIRUS INFECTS BESTSELLERS" (October 1990) By PATTI WICKER

Bestsellers are falling victim to a strange computer virus that mysteriously injects fragments of nonsensical and perverse poetry into the computer files of bestseller manuscripts. And soon "NO book will be safe from this dastardly infection." Or so claims the proud carrier and self-professed connoisseur of dormant diseases, Rollo Whitehead.

Rollo Whitehead, now 65 years old, has for years been investigating dormant diseases like feline leukemia, diseases that hitch rides on the infected being's DNA for generations, even centuries, and then suddenly become activated at certain moments in time, usually during some severe moment of world anxiety such as World War II.

42 years ago Rollo Whitehead was anything but a medical researcher. He was known back then as the shepherd of a ragtag flock of would-be bards called the Beatniks. But early on he distanced himself from these "Wannabeats," as he's so fond of calling them, by "refusing to participate in their ego shenanigans and media brokering because," Whitehead explains during our exclusive phone conversation with him, "all they so desperately sought was the approval of the very normals they publicly denounced!"

He even went so far as to refuse to publish his poems, insisting it was as "distasteful as exchanging valises of dutch beef." And then he irked the rest of them by refusing to even write them down. This he decided after having his cluttered Greenwich Village garret ransacked a number of times back in the free-love 60s by those "seeking remunerative inspiration." Some of these stolen manuscripts later reappeared mysteriously as the Beatnik classics *On The Road* by Jean Kerouac and *Howl* by Allen Ginsberg. Or so Whitehead insists. Since then he has committed any and everything to "the safe deposit box of my memory."

Safe until now that is. With the advent of personal computers came a whole new world of recordkeeping and information processing. With it also came the "barnacles clinging to the ship of inspiration", the various hackers and software scofflaws who took Rollo Whitehead as their mentor when some of Whitehead's "Poems & Fragments" inadvertently found their way into the re-issue files of Pocket Book Publishing in 1980.

How this happened is still a mystery. And if Whitehead has any clues he isn't talking. No one, including experts in computer virology, seems sure. Some think it may have been a telephone modem, or a prankster, editorial error or computer virus. The lines "brilliant swerving flecks of steam / hissing low like satyrs / come and smally / lift and silky / blow a hambone," appeared as if by miracle, amongst the pages of *The Pocket Aristotle*, like "leaf blight on a rose bush," Whitehead muses.

The second incident occurred a year later when more of Whitehead's self-described "post-sensical verse infections" found their way into the worldwide bestseller, *THE ROCKEFELLERS: An American Dynasty*. He is flattered and amused but really not all that surprised. "Viruses of all kinds are very wily, adaptable buggers."

Other authors victimized by Whitehead's "mysterious verse infections" are Barbara Cartland, Donald Trump, Nancy Reagan and Stephen King. Although, in the case of King, no one really noticed until 4 years after *The Shining* was first published! Whitehead chuckles but insists there is "no secret. It merely happens. Like weather. Like a bowel movement."

These events, these seeming miraculous infections, have sent shock waves through the entire publishing industry. It left editors, typesetters and proofreaders alike, shellshocked and miffed. Whitehead's infections have led to various national information industry legislation, the tightening of entrance codes, the re-thinking of security systems for the nation's entire information and intelligence communities. And, along with that, the advent of an entire new industry, Software doctors, security technology and computer anti-virus specialists.

"Way I look at it, I'm the best thing that ever happened to some of these books and certainly the best stimulus to come along in the software industry in a long time."

6. "MILLIONAIRE BEATS NO LONGER BURN GREENBACKS" (September 1982) By LOTTY LABOUCHE

List reveals slumming lifestyles of The Beat & Heinous. No Bowery Bums these mega-bards of brokered novel and the leveraged lyrics:

1. Jack Kerouac: First brooding hunk super model. He was to Wrangler jeans what the Marlboro Man is to Marlboro cigarettes. Estate net worth: **$128 million.**

2. Jack Micheline: He added an 'E' to his last name to distance himself from French tire empire, Michelin. Net worth: **$86 million.**

3. William Burroughs: Claims to have scandalized his way out of inheritance as an heir to Burroughs Machine Corp. wealth. But he hired Saatchi & Saatchi to manufacture his beat image at great expense, $1.5 million. Net worth **$72.5 million.**

4. Gary Snyder: Lives comfortably on $45,000 "monthly allowance" he receives from his early investments in his father's Monsanto chemical and paper corporation based on his investment and aerobic regimen called Zen & The Art of Financial Management (which he now teaches at Naropa). Net worth **$44.4 million.**

5. Joyce Johnson: Is no minor character when it comes to the heart (and wallet) of 'Daddy Chembucks' Don Johnson, chairman of Johnson & Johnson. She writes many more checks than books. Net worth **$33.7 million.**

6. Diane DiPrima: Leggy and comely beatnik princess is actually the director of the chain of Arthur Murray-Douglas DiPrima Jitterbug Dance & Jazz Poetry Studios. Net worth including real estate, **$26.3 million.**

7. Ferlinghetti, Huncke, Clellon Holmes: founders of a repossession agency and law firm specializing in Bebop royalty cases, Ferlinghetti, Huncke & Holmes created a special niche & have for their surviving heirs created an estate with estimated assets in excess of **$18.6 million.**

8. Amiri Baraka: In partnership with ex-Black Panther Eldridge Cleaver, Baraka created a fashion empire with his "Sighmaster," sexy orthopedic hot pants for men. Net worth **$14.9 million.**

9. Gregory Corso: Mastermind of the very trendy Corso Torso line of rebuilt corsets & lingerie has recently added the MD-20-20 & Radical Chic lines of repossessed vintage undergarments. A true rags to riches story. Net worth **$13.3 million.**

10. John Giorno: Maven behind Giorno Poetry Systems has moved from messages on record discs to messages in a bottle. Because of a recent deal with Snapple Beverages consumers can now find "pithy re-bopped poesie" nuggets under the caps of all Snapple beverages. Net worth **$12.45 million.**

CARL WATSON

IN THE PURSUIT OF MEANING, WE FIND ONLY TRENDS

I Suffer from a Profound Misunderstanding of Spontaneous Prose

The year was 1993, in the early years of a prolonged emotional and economic recession. Rummaging through the discount bin of 20th century aesthetics, looking for a movement to glom onto, desperate sycophants and trend spotters alike found themselves engaged in attempts to escape what seemed an indigenous 'culture of complaint.' Apparently things weren't going well in the 20th century and people needed something to say about it.

What a lot of people were complaining about was the increasing dilution of all meaning in life coupled with a general watered-down value system (aesthetic and moral) of which one archaic beast known as 'Spontaneous Prose' stood out as a prime example, for reasons beyond the obvious canonization of the Beats and their subsequent market value as retro *'nostalgique du jour.'* Because of the increased slack it added to the collective facial features, the question arose in academic circles as to whether it was an aesthetic statement of individualism, or a social disease on the level of 'Art for Arts Sake,' etc.

Of course, to truly understand the Spontaneous Prose phenomenon it was necessary for researchers to review its precedents and disguises. Technically of course they were speaking of the old internal monologue, automatic writing and stream of consciousness—stylistic pretenses based on a free associative process which blatantly denied the rhetorical links between intent and action, a kind of brain jazz, thought scum, or mental masturbation staining the bedsheets so to speak of contemporary literary complacency.

And while every picture tells a story, every handle also has a twist. Automatic writing, for instance, caused one to think of automatic weapons—that is something connected to the subconscious that could kill, or perhaps, illuminate the user (death and illumination being linked, as per the old adage, to see god is to die.) It was as if those images born in the brain were like guns to be used against the thinker—a difficult path to creativity, as well as the underpinning of the surrealist notion of violent beauty, it lent a certain amount of aggression to inanimate thoughts, helping to create the violent society which dominated the end of the 1900s.

Stream of consciousness, on the other hand was just that —a stream, whose currents were subject to all sorts of historical detritus, a contrived set of quotation marks, which enabled the scribbler to pass off heavily edited material as if it were something some character had actually thought. Common sense however belies the idea of 'thought' altogether and eventually let the wind out of this particular bag of fun.

Now it is common knowledge today that complete sentences are indeed anathema to the visual mind, no one actually thinks in sentences, or even in coherent sequences —we constantly contradict ourselves—this truth never faded the enthusiasm of Spontaneous Prose advocates however who consistently banked on its seemingly endless parenthetical powers, as opposed, to say, veering off into hi-brow realms of suggestive understatement, irony or some other demanding literary device.

Part of the problem with and the popularity of Spontaneous Prose was that people actually did believe in it (eagerly disguising its therapeutic intent as literary invention) ranting on and on and on in public about nothing, under what could only be called a faux-formalistic gloss, a patina of significance and theory.

Thus the endless pages of Spontaneous tomes like *Desolation Angels,* which purported to plow new prosaic turf ended up like so much rusted farm machinery in the literary gully, dangerous toys for children, whereupon an aimless student population was deterred from higher pursuits and baited toward some pseudo prima materia, the watered down psychological ur-soup of an exhausted, flatulent and overeducated society, squatting bloated at a cultural banquet table at which was being served the sacrificial lamb chops of an anesthetized, antibiotic-ridden herd of consumers who preened themselves before the mercantile gun of 'literature,' which at the time could as well have been a camera, or it could be merely the next jazzy new product.

One may well ask: What true intellectual could witness this rancid fat dripping from the cheeks of the academics and not be made sick by it? But by then intellectualism was already condemned to proselytizing and the concept of confession pretty much continued to define the literary climate of the 80s and 90s.

Indeed, such self-indulgence gave the go ahead to generations of writers to gaze lovingly in the muddled mirror of their own minds and believe there was something there other than the jargon that had been fed to them in the form of infectious jingles, buzz phrases and the general sloganeering which they could not seem to divorce from their own *fin de siècle* thought processes.

The whole issue not only gets confusing but fails to resolve the question as to whether Spontaneous Prose was a literary testament to 'real time' or (in psychoanalytic jargon) a form of 'primary thought' captured and crystallized by the fame motive. And of course there were those who held that all Spontaneous Prose is at inception bastardized by intent (like the subatomic particle, or instance of behavior, that is altered in the act of observation). That is, can one think "I am writing Spontaneous Prose at this time," and still be writing spontaneous prose. And does not the desire to write good prose immediately affect the pretense.

After all, if one wishes to write 'good' Spontaneous Prose (a subjective value judgment to be sure) one automatically negates the spontaneity of the writing altogether—the mediocrity factor is built right in—leaving us with a literary device containing the seeds of its own disvalue, and as well coming dangerously close to glossolalia and other fundamentalist enslavement tricks, phenomenon which outside academic frameworks would most certainly be labeled pathological if not right wing extremist. A circle turns like a carousel in the dark night of human aesthetics. A target with the dignity of the soul at the bullseye center.

The following is a confession of a Spontaneous Prose dabbler, interviewed at the Neil Cassady Center hospital for the Literary Infirm.

I Tried to Write Spontaneous Prose but All I Ever Got was Tired

Never a spontaneous person to begin with, I've lived most of my life as an afterthought, trying to catch up with my own *a posteriori* ambitions. I never questioned the notion that meaning was achieved through retroaction and deferral. In other words, I steadfastly held to the belief that nothing means. In fact I've always felt rigorous discipline was necessary to control all the hate, falsity, rationalization that passes for meaning. Meaning is/was never more than desire and propaganda forced into proximity with economics.

I must admit of course, I have used the device myself as an engine when needed to generate pages of 'fluff'. One might say at those moments I was guilty of having taken a job in a sweat shop of prosaic production where the paycheck was minute. And as the previous sentence might hint, I did find the spontaneous method an excellent technique for writing letters, because I usually don't have that much to say, even to my friends, especially those whom I've not seen in some time, so it fills up the page and presents the illusion of 'interest' or 'caring' or 'communication' all of which are valuable when trying to talk someone you never see out of a couple dollars from a distance of hundreds, even thousands of miles.

It's all basically relative to what one wants to believe. Anyway, arriving at the above 'truth' via the very process I intended to condemn spurred me on to further investigations into the relationship of intent and act, paradox and absurdity. Thus I decided to approach my next exercise in Spontaneous Prose like an adventure in altered states of consciousness, nudging the Internal Monologue along with various chemicals, figuring not only to illustrate reality's fragile tone, but more pompously, the fact that history itself must necessarily be based on the mood of the moment—making Spontaneous Prose in its political portent an effective mode of global perspective manipulation, whereby some juvenile power broker somewhere might spontaneously say "Hey lets go to war," and the plebeian masses would make it so.

Thus it was I opened my vast medicine chest to explore the consequences. One night after a particularly rich Spontaneous Cocktail I remember waking up at 2 am with my head resting on the computer keyboard. I had passed out and consequently typed fifteen pages of semi-colons—appropriately obscure and misunderstood modes of punctuation—with nary a clause to justify them. It was an apt metaphor for my life, but I wouldn't call it truth. Looking for an alibi for my lethargy, I took stock of the empty pill bottles that littered the floor. I was forced to note that most of my Spontaneous Prose aids had actually been depressants, whose prime purpose was not augmentation, but its opposite, that is to turn off the Spontaneous Prose switch in my impoverished head. It was time to rethink my approach. This took several weeks of intense procrastination.

In fact I spent so long studying and preparing for my session of Spontaneous Prose that I never achieved it, that is I weighed carefully all the possible yeahs and neahs, the do's and don'ts, etc, until the act of prosody itself became a mute issue, barely separable from my minute-to-minute life. I did not know however if this was a confirmation or a denial of its aesthetic validity, but it also seemed to not matter, as slowly, very slowly my very life itself was being unwittingly 'framed' so to speak by its own unstructured narrative. I became frightened, I saw Spontaneous Prose bursting forth everywhere, pompously, like a hydra-headed flower, the unchained psychobabble of the universe itself, disjointed and logical, silly and significant at the same time. Indeed the concept had become some sort of revelatory Beast of

Babylon roaming around in my pre-subconscious with a typewriter and an editing knife. I found myself looking at every situation as a possible narrative interjection or aside, perhaps even the subject of an entire novel (*à la* Proust). I could not type as fast as the spontaneous prose in my head demanded. I could not sort out the thoughts, one from the other, much less which to keep and which to toss, as I had no way of knowing what was valid, true, pretty, insightful, brilliant, or simply rubbish.

True the whole experience leant a certain air of cosmic whimsy to life, but I also had to face the fact that I'd spent the better part of my life trying to escape precisely that whimsical entombment. The ritualistic nature of the spontaneous act had become oppressive to the nth degree. A simple literary contrivance had actually become a fascist state in which the most meaningless of utterances and animal cries was not only ascribed prosaic value, but outright godhead.

The intensity of this unwanted spiritual life drove me into a corner. Random thoughts assembled themselves out of the zeitgeist at breakneck speed. I let these thoughts become the animals they were, attempting to fix them with the nail gun of my so-called 'talent.' It was a sad sight to see: a grungy, beaten hunter in a forest of hackneyed signs, gunning for any old sequence of syllables out of pure semantic desperation. If I managed to tack something to the wall like a trophy I only ended up validating that old crucifixion equation which ends every sentence with doubt. Thus it was I cried out in the silence of my heretical night "Oh Jack, oh Allen, why has thou forsaken me."

As a young literary wanna-be and vision-seeker, I used to wake myself up during dream states in order to write down the unformed gibberish that passed through my mind as intense pure language. But what I actually achieved was a state of perpetual wakefulness, in which I was so severely self-monitored, so engaged, I could not sleep more than a minute or two without having to record the passage of some nugget of truth or other. A similar thing happened under the dictatorship of Spontaneous Prose, that is I *monitored* myself to the point I was no longer living in the 'spontaneous' world, but another world, one in which I second guessed myself right out of experience, and into existential boredom. And there was little comfort in the feeling of community there, let me tell you.

And I'm not talking about your be-bop daddy-o's whistling dixie at the funeral of free thought—no. I'm not talking about your protobeat bodhisatva muscle boys drinking coffee in the all night diners of America, waxing romantic on the divinity of the mundane—no. I'm talking about a sickness and alienation that began back when the sons of east coast intellectual privilege first doffed their tweeds and went riding off into a fabled and romanticized 'West' in search of clichés.

And, okay, I admit I drove that car of Spontaneous Prose myself for what seemed several metaphorical years and all I ever got was confused. Indeed the very notion of pan-directional beatitude, like the overdeveloped American freeway system itself, seemed to be absenting the literary heart from the human hierarchy—it gave us the illusion of motion but it left us flaccid, as the bookshelves of our nation strained under the weight of small talk and idealess mush, the babble of millions of so-called individuals, whose sole voice and validity was based on the fact that they, yes they themselves existed and were people too, yes the entire world was free to be you and me —individuals, okay—but in the quest for that individuality we had become blathering saps, spouting poetry in boxing rings and accepting plaudits for hard won 'feelings' that we probably didn't even have. Walking bags of gibberish, self-reflection and double-talk, we the idle mush-mouthed masses had at last been tamed by publishing house titans, we'd had the fiber processed right out of our verbal cream of wheat.

As Anita Bryant might have said had she been a literary critic "Milquetoast, it isn't just for breakfast anymore."

Conclusion

I am reminded of the anecdote of the child in an art therapy class I once sat in on. This naive child believed she had so many thoughts she had to keep her hands pressed against her head to hold them in. She walked around with her hands on her head saying "I have too many thoughts. Somebody please help me." Well, no one did. And although

I was no child myself, my head too had become just this sort of arrogant balloon, my features expanding until I was incapable of any kind of expression whatsoever, except perhaps raw fear. Eventually however, the cause behind the gesture subtly changed. Friends commented on the fact that as I walked about with my hands over my eyes and ears, it appeared I was trying to shut the world out, not hold it in. At first I denied this accusation. Then one day I saw myself in the mirror and realized what I had become and that's when I started to drink. And thank god for that.

I eventually freed myself from the bonds of Spontaneous Prose, and all its evolutionarily challenged cousins. I am free to once again pursue the twisted overwrought Victorian labyrinths of formal language, be it laden with cultural bias or what have you. Once again the universe is a tidy place for me, the Borgesian Library where things have meaning, even if they do have no substance. Once upon a time the Cheshire Cat of Alice in Wonderland warned the pilgrim protagonist of that ground-breaking novel "Go not that way, that way madness lies." Immediately afterwards, the old cat disappears. 100 years later, marketing man Allen Ginsberg, started an early version of his infamous beat anthem *Howl* with the words "I have seen the best minds of my generation destroyed by Spontaneous Prose." And now we know only too well—this was no reflection, it was a prophecy.

JEROME SALA

BEATNIK STANZAS

"words like *light, dark, night, star, vision, dream, angel, haunted, mad, sad, gone,* etc., are repeated by these authors until they take on the power of a litany."
Gerard Nicosia, *Memory Babe*

1.
I was a gone star then,
but my bongos drove me mad—
my bebop angel walked me to the light
of a haunted abstract painting:
its spidery drips recalled the night
my vision darkened
and I threw away my turtleneck
in a dream

2.
when my visionary gym shoes squeak
on this sad floor,
I get mad at the angel
who cut off my goatee
while I was dreaming
of a haunted coffee house:
there the gloomy dark night
once lightened up on me
and I could see the stars
once more

3.
like night, my vision is haunted;
Charlie Parker has gone back to the stars
and the fireflies light their mad tails
in honor of the sad, angelic moths—
problem is, every time I close my eyes
vision vanishes and the dream world
takes over

4.
Zen is neither dark nor light
but it is sad:
no madness
no angels
no vision
no dreams
no stars
no gone daddios
no haunted lightning
no nights no black arts
no Jean Paul Sartre

5.
my angel doesn't believe in Christmas
but he sent me a roll of toilet paper to type on
anyway—
he's so gone, he caters to the stars in my eyes—
he knows my sad nights
long for the light of his dark feet
across my dreamy pad:
my vision is about all I live for
and this drives me mad

6.
if you were still a mad poet
I would haunt you — a washed up angel
if you were still a dark vision
I would throw my life away
in search of your gone light

if you were still awake
I would walk you back to dream land
if you suddenly went sane
I would drive you mad all over again
but now that you've turned square
I must build you back to hip stardom
and this is a sad, sad task

7.
...so then the old beat angel barged into the party, complaining that its sad monotony only gained grace from the
dead genius that haunted its banal vision.

The newbeat angel threw water in his face. He explained
that spontaneity is the child of a humdrum father. That the
light arises only from darkness. That dreams are born from
rational days — like madness from sanity — like the stars on
an empty night, when all the celebrities have gone home...

LIZ RESKO

THE HUNDRED-AND-FIRST POEM
FROM THE CHINESE

Scott Street was looking bleak at that hour.

Very few cars or pedestrians ventured out in the rain
and the only light on the street was from the shops still open;
the deli on the corner, and of course the record store.

I walked towards the yellow, bleary light and the soft keening
sound coming from the shop. Climbing the stairs, the creak-
    ing mildewed stairs
I felt very old. The smell of the storm, the rotten wood, the
    damp scarf presses on me.
Ken said I could crash at his place — the door is open, just
    don't let the cat out.

Dictionaries everywhere—in boxes, on tables crammed in drawers.
Notebooks with scrawled Chinese characters, Japanese
    ideograms covered the floor.
The cat stepped over them lightly and cried for food.
I open a can of something, creamed corn, I think, and dump
    it into her bowl.

I light the gas stove for warmth and open the oven door. My
    glasses fog.
I grab a notebook and read.
I cannot read Chinese but the characters speak to me.
    Maybe it's the wind, screeching through

the wooden shingles that inspires me (or maybe it's because
     there's no T.V. or radio anywhere in
sight) but I find myself drawn to the works of a little known
     poetess from the 9th century.
I pick up the big red book, an index of Chinese radicals, and
     I begin my translation.

A few hour later, bleary-eyed, I have a poem:

THE DAY OF COLD COFFEE

On the day of Cold Coffee
I walked along the East River
The boats with their waving flags
And the floating debris:
Plastic bags, beer cans,
Cardboard cups like little lanterns
Called to me.
"Little Sister, do not be afraid,
Another year has passed
And we are still here,
Floating like a lotus.
And you are still
Watching from above."

SUSAN SCUTTI

MUTE SKY

By the time I finished Bowles it was midnight. Kit's life added up in a two plus two kind of way until she's the one who goes mad in the end and wanders away from her own salvation. For a long time after I finished reading I lay curled like a question mark on my couch. Unwilling to sleep, I smoked and wondered if my own life was progressing in the same arithmetic way toward an equally obvious sum.

When I finally got into bed, I didn't turn off the light. I wanted to call the man I'd slept with the night before but I didn't. I thought he would think I was needy.

The night before I had felt the sensation of his hand along my skin and somewhere above it as well. In that moment, it felt like I actually had a soul and my soul was a shell surrounding my body and his hand was touching my skin and my spirit simultaneously. Streetlight entered the room and touched his pale skin: in this halflight he looked featureless, like hope. I felt a long wrinkle in the sheet along my back.

In the morning I left the bed to make coffee. For a minute I watched the flames stroking the bottom of the kettle then I went back to him in my bed. When I looked at him I knew my eyes must look soft and touched because he looked away from me as if I was asking for something.

After he left, I saw my curtains still open, I saw the sky beyond them, and suddenly I was reminded of the room where I had lived alone for the first time in my life. I shed my virginity there. Tenderly, he touched me; how simple my fear of him was. Afterwards, we said goodbye and he quietly closed the door behind him. For a moment, I looked through the window at the mute sky then I lay on my bed, as long and narrow as a coffin.

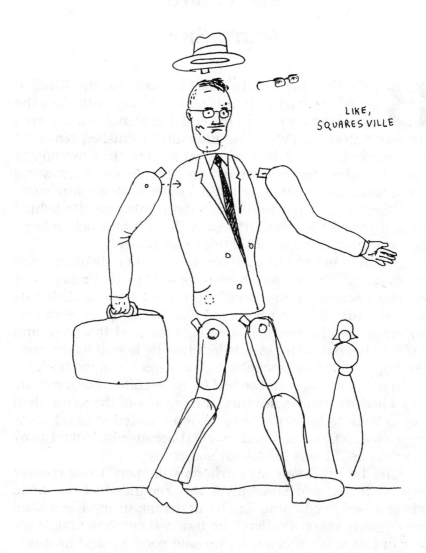

LIKE,
SQUARES VILLE

ELIZABETH MORSE

THE NAKED, THE DEAD AND THE UNEMPLOYED

I met Norman Mailer during the Reagan era recession of 1982 when I was dating a friend of his who I'll call Larry. What Larry and I had in common was that we were both in danger of losing our jobs. He was an encyclopedia sales-man whose sales volume had gone way down, and I was an editor at a management consulting firm whose job was being phased out.

"I sell books to shmucks," Larry told me over sandwiches and beer. "But I'm not making any money. I'd try selling shmucks to books, but I don't think the books would have them." This view of customers may have at least partially explained why he wasn't making any money.

Larry had acted in a play with Mailer's wife, Norris. That's how he knew Mailer.

When he'd told me about this friendship, it scared me. But I was also impressed. Mailer was the celebrated author who was alleged to have stabbed one of his earlier wives. I'd been assigned to read a book of his in college, which had turned out to be a combination of male supremacist curses and intriguing incantations.

Before this, I'd thought that Larry was a nice but fairly ordinary guy who'd take me out to a movie every Saturday night in his Upper East Side neighborhood. Afterwards we went back to his studio apartment and listened to new age chimes on the stereo.

Even though he complained about his mounting credit card debt, new furnishings appeared in his apartment every week. Once it was speakers that looked like a folding screen. Another time it was a bigger bed.

"I'm really very fond of Norman," Larry said. "If he wanted me to hide Jack Abbott in my apartment, I would do it."

This was a surprise. The week before he'd been telling me he'd been listening through the wall to the man in the next apartment. Larry feared that this guy was in the mafia. I didn't know about Larry, but I didn't want to share the fate of the waiter at the Binibon.

"Here," Larry said, handing me a book of Norman's poetry. "Read some of these."

I started to read, and the words really stayed with me. At least his dislike of women wasn't obvious here. Since I was struggling to write my own poetry, I decided he wasn't a bad role model.

A few weeks later, Larry invited me to Norris Mailer's art opening at a Soho restaurant. I was thrilled.

By this time, I'd started a new job at a bank. Since the opening was on a weeknight, I felt compelled to wear a suit as many women were starting to do in the 1980s even though I was afraid a suit would make me look more feminist that Mailer would like.

When I got there, the paintings were odd portraits of 1950s women in harlequin glasses. Norris Mailer, a former model, had beautiful auburn hair, but her face looked sharp and pinched. Who knew how Norman was treating her?

Larry was faced with the unpleasant prospect of having to ask for a job. He, too, was wearing a suit. Since it was raining, he'd rubberbanded plastic food storage bags over his shoes. His credit cards were maxed out so he couldn't afford boots.

Larry led me directly to Norman, and described a reading and performance series Larry and I were planning to hold in public libraries. Afterwards, Norman slapped Larry's back and said, "The impresario!" Standing together, they looked like Laurel and Hardy.

After introducing me to both Norman and Norris, Larry started talking to Norman in low tones. Without knowing what he was saying, I knew he was begging for work.

As soon as Norman left, Larry said, "He wants me to be his secretary in his Brooklyn Heights apartment."

"Well," I said, "it's a definite salary. You haven't been earning much in commissions lately."

"But I can't do that!" He waved his arms wildly. "I used to run a department before I went back to sales! I used to have a secretary!"

"Maybe it's better than the usual secretarial work."

"Norman wants me to do typing and photocopying. That's what he said. How can he expect me to do that?"

"Maybe that's all he has available."

"But he's Norman Mailer!" Larry said. "He should be able to create a job! He's capable of anything and everything. Think of the things he's done! Think of the books he's written!"

While I shuddered to think of Larry's overbearing debt, I have to say I was relieved that we wouldn't be hiding Jack Abbott any time soon.

KEVIN RIORDAN

SCREAMS FROM THE MAD-DADDY HOUSE — ERGO COGITO AND THE SHRINERS

The record you hold in your mitts is the end product of an almost inchoate, incomprehensible (you still with me?) set of circumstances that would defy description by any sane jazz aficionado. This round, black artifact has been extruded down, down a long, darkling, fertile chute of muscular, meaty endgame thereness. I'm talking about life. This is arguably the very first record by an artist, of whatever pointy headed, lung-dead, hung-up generation, who was literally *bred to bop.* When young Ergo Cogito first showed signs of a precocious proclivity towards music at the tender age of two, his ultrahip, with-it, *natural* parents put him on a strict audio diet. They spoke to him only in *vout.* Having observed that all the jazz greats of yesteryear sounded an awful lot alike, the Cogitos had junior listening to train wrecks, sirens, sound effects, language instruction reels played bassackwards, anything but music. A typical Sunday would have them driving out to the airport to listen to jets take off, a visit to the scrapyard where junk cars were cubed, a picnic under the elevated tracks, where they turned a sharp corner, then back home to work out on his baritone ax. Eventually, he began collecting platters on his own, but he compulsively customized them. He'd take, say, an Ornette Coleman side and re-groove it with his finenibbed woodburning pen, rearranging the solos to hop all over the place, gently warping it to round out a phrase that was just too damn straight. His parents' Grundig console was rewired through a voltage regulator automatically compensating the speed to play entire platters at the same pitch. *Take the A Train* lasted two hours but the very same train G-bound only took ten minutes! He also tried spinning sandpaper discs, pizza cardboards and berets, with varying results. It was only a matter of time before he attracted an appropriate group of sidemen. Those ignobles of the mystic shrine are surely *it*. Riding around in midget cars over bubble wrap and broken glass while wailing on upside down instruments is not something you're born with, unless your mama was struck by lightning while you were gestating.

So platter players of the world, forewarned is four-armed. Carefully insert the needle into the groove, do whatever it takes to relax your musculature, and tiptoe to a place of safety to fully savor and *dig*est the sounds of *Screams...*

TULI KUPFERBERG

MINOR POET FROM THE LOWER EAST SIDE

(tune: Slum Goddess from the Lower East Side)

Well, I wandered lonely 'nto a bar one day
Who did I hear having his say?
Minor poet from the Lower East Side
Minor poet don't got no goddamn pride

Well the first time that I heard him he addled my brain
The next time that I saw him nearly drove me insane
The third time he got me he trapped me in a corner
The last time that he rapped me I thot I was a goner
Minor poet from the Lower East Side
Minor poet aint got no goddamn pride

Well this poet from hell — hey who cd he be?
I looked in the window wowwwww — turned out to be ME!
I cdnt believe it — I fell on the floor
Praying stop me lord before I read some more!

Minor poet from the Lower East Side
Minor poet got no goddamn pride
Minor poet from the Lower East Side
Minor poet aint got no goddamn pride
I'm gonna commit poe c i d e
I better commit poecide

JOSE PADUA

GIANT STEPS
(THE BIRTH OF THE FUGS)

They were called X-Ray Specs — put them on and the world became a see-though paradise. You'd always see ads for them in the back pages of magazines like *True Detective*, *Argosy*, or *Nugget*...right next to the ads for the sea monkeys. But while the sea monkeys were an obvious rip-off, the X-Ray Specs you weren't so sure about. And looking at the crude drawing in the ad of some X-Ray bespectacled hipster smiling from sideburn to sideburn as he sees right through this curvy broad's party dress put dirty thoughts in your head: what if they really worked? If they did, it would be well worth the money.

Which is exactly what Ed Sanders thought when he ordered them in the spring of 1964. Ed was just a horny young poet back then; and although he had a fat notebook full of empty pages ready to receive his blank verse, he had no receptacles, other than his hairy right hand, through which to relieve his innate horniness. So naturally, when he opened up his mailbox one day at two in the afternoon to see that his pair of X-Ray Specs had arrived, he smiled — that sideburn-to-sideburn smile.

"Ah yes," he said to himself, "the real fucky fucky."

Ed immediately headed toward Washington Square Park which he thought would be as good a place as any to try them out. But on the way he had a thought.

"I'll show them to Tuli," he said, again talking to himself — in those days he was always talking to himself. "It'll impress the shit out of him."

The man Ed wanted to impress was Tuli Kupferberg, who at that time was already something of a fixture on the Village scene. Ed looked up to Tuli. Tuli was older, more experienced, and seemed to know just about everything. But this pair of X-Ray Specs, Ed was sure, would take him completely by surprise.

Ed got to Tuli's apartment and knocked. Wrapped in a brown army blanket and wearing a two day growth of stubble on his chin, Tuli answered the door. He'd just woken up.

"Look what I got," Ed blurted out.

"What the fuck?" Tuli grumbled, rubbing the sleep from his eyes. He slouched over to get a closer look at the pair of X-Ray Specs Ed held out proudly with both hands. "So you got some fruity looking shades. Big fucking deal. I'm going back to sleep."

"These aren't *shades*, man" Ed argued. "These are fucking X-Ray Specs. They're the real thing, man — *the real fucky fucky*."

"The real fucky fucky?"

"Shit, Tuli, you know what I mean."

Tuli grabbed them and was about to put them on when Ed stopped him.

"Don't look at *me* with those things," Ed snapped. "Let's go to the park. Let's try looking at some *gurls* with these things."

"Girls," Tuli mumbled. "Oh, okay...girls."

Tuli got dressed, then he and Ed walked to Washington Square Park, the X-Ray Specs burning a hole in Ed's shirt pocket. When they got to the park, it was crowded; lots of people, lots of *girls*. They sat on a bench facing the arch, the sun bearing down brightly upon them

"Okay," Tuli said, "give them to me. I get to try them on first."

Ed pulled them from his pocket and handed them to Tuli. Tuli opened them up and with an exaggerated flourish put them over his eyes.

"Holy fucking shit!" he exclaimed. "Everyone is fucking naked. And that girl over there, see her? She's got tattoos of flames shooting out from around her nipples. And that guy over there...he's got *two* dicks. What a bunch of fucking freaks!"

"Lemme see, lemme see!" Ed shouted.

"No, wait. And that lady over there. She's got a shaved pussy...nice...real nice...And that girl over there too. And that girl..."

"Let me see, let me see," Ed yelled, trying to grab them from Tuli's head.

Tuli pulled away and stood up, doing a 360-degree turn as he gazed all around the park.

"I have seen the best bodies of my generation STARK FUCKING NAKED."

He pulled the X-Ray Specs from his face, bowed, then threw them to Ed, who immediately put them on. Ed looked all around. He looked up, then down. He looked around again.

"What the fuck? I don't see anything. Everything just looks fuzzy and dark."

"What did you expect?" Tuli said. "You got ripped off."

"Shit," Ed cried, "fucking shit."

He dropped the X-Ray Specs to the ground and was about to stomp on them when Tuli stopped him.

"Don't do *that*," Tuli said, "I think I can do something useful with those things." He stood up. "Come on, Ed, let's check out the situation here."

Tuli led Ed around the park as he carefully studied everyone. Finally he pointed out a guy playing a guitar.

"See that guy over there?" he said.

"Yeah,"

"Well, come on over. And play along with this. Or better yet just keep quiet."

When they got close it was apparent that the guy playing guitar was fucked up. *Totally fucked up.*

"Sounding pretty good there, kid," Tuli said.

The kid, who seemed to be around Ed's age, looked up at Tuli and widened his eyes.

"Oh...uh...thanks," the kid said.

"Do you know what these are?" Tuli asked, holding out the pair of X-Ray Specs.

The kid studied them for a minute, squinting, then said, "No, whazzat?"

"These, my friend, are X-Ray Specs — the greatest invention of the twentieth century." Tuli paused a moment and then added, "They're the real fucky fucky."

"The real fucky fucky? Izzat so?"

"It is so. Me and my young friend Ed here have been in the park all afternoon checking out the girls with these things. Looking not only at their faces and their legs, but their *entire nude bodies*. Because when you put these on my friend, you can see right through their clothing."

"Izzat so?'

"It is so. Totally nude girls...Do you like girls?"

"Why, yeah. I shure do."

"Do you like naked girls?"

"Why, yes shure, I do," the kid answered, sitting up straight.

"Well, then, try these on. I think you'll like what you see."

Tuli gently placed the X-Ray Specs over the kid's eyes. Before the kid could even begin to look around Tuli began to shout:

"CAN YOU FUCKING BELIEVE IT? Look at that beautiful girl over there with the polka dots tattooed all over her tits and belly. And that girl over there with the blue and yellow stripes tattooed all over her body. Looks almost like she's wearing a dress, but she's not, she's NUDE. Totally NUDE!"

"Holy shit!" the kid exclaimed, his mouth agape

"But don't leave them on too long," Tuli warned, pulling them off the kid's head. "You have to let your eyes get accustomed to these glasses before you leave them on too long. But once your eyes get used to them you can wear them all the time."

"Izzat so?"

"It is so."

The kid shook his head in amazement.

"Damn those are some fucken great glasses. Where can I get a pair?"

"In Europe," Tuli explained. "France, to be specific — you know how those French people are. They invented the French kiss, the French post card, the French tickler, and now this. But it costs the equivalent of about $300 on the French black market. That's the only place you can get them."

"Damn, I wish I could get me a pair."

"Well, I can sell you this pair for $300."

"Shit, I ain't got no $300."

"Oh, that's too bad." Tuli scratched his chin. "But hey, that's a nice guitar you got there."

"Oh yeah?"

"Damn nice guitar...I'll tell you what. I'll trade you this here pair of X-Ray Specs for that there guitar."

"Oh yeah?"

"Sure thing."

"Well, shit yeah. Cool," the kid said. "Here take it."

He handed the guitar to Tuli who promptly handed it to Ed.

"Thanks," Tuli said. "And for you, my friend, your very own pair of X-Ray Specs — direct from France."

He handed the X-Ray Specs to the kid as he and Ed started backing away.

"Don't try them on again just yet. Better let your eyes rest for a few more minutes. Then just let yourself go crazy looking at those naked girls."

"OKAY!," the kid shouted.

"Just think bare breasts," Tuli added as he backed further away.

"Yeah."

"And bare asses."

"Yeah!"

"And pussy."

"Fuck yeah!"

Tuli and Ed quickly walked away. When they were out of the kid's sight, Ed turned admiringly to Tuli.

"Damn, Tuli, that was *smooth.*"

"It was nothing, Ed. The kid was totally fucked up. It was like robbing a crippled dwarf with a Sherman tank."

"But still, it was cool."

"Nope. The cool part's coming up. Because now you're finally going to get yourself some girls. Really naked girls."

"But how?"

Tuli pointed to the guitar.

"With *that*," he said.

"How's that going to get me some girls?"

"Don't you understand? Do I have to explain everything, Ed?" Tuli shook his head, amazed that his young friend still didn't get it. "That's a guitar. It makes music. And you know those poems you've been writing? Well, to tell you the truth, they don't hold up very well by themselves. They won't get you any accolades from the beatniks. And they sure as hell won't get you any pussy. Which is where the guitar comes in."

Ed scratched his head.

"You mean, like, turn my poems into songs?"

"Now you're getting it. Though now that I think of it, you and a guitar isn't quite enough. You'll never make it as a solo act. You're going to need a whole *band*."

"A band?"

"That's right. Shit, I'll even help you out. I know a couple of other guys. We can all be in your band."

Ed shook his head.

"Still, I wished those X-Ray Specs worked."

"You *still* don't get it," Tuli said, raising his voice. "You see, when you're in a band, girls will undress for you. *You won't have to see through anything.*"

Ed walked along in silence. They were on Sixth Avenue now, making their way back to Tuli's apartment. Tuli looked straight ahead, thinking. He was always thinking. He began to walk more rapidly, rubbing the stubble on his chin, when he heard a voice a few paces behind him. A young voice. The voice of a kid experiencing his first sense of revelation, his first understanding of the world and how it worked.

"Oh...I GET IT!" Ed shouted to himself.

And on hearing this Tuli felt old, very old. And while Ed was having his first sense of revelation, Tuli was having his first real sense of sadness. He picked up his pace even more, then suddenly stopped until Ed was again walking by his side. After a moment Tuli smiled. But his smile was nothing like that of the hipster in the ad for the X-Ray Specs. It was nothing like the smile Ed was now wearing smugly on his face. It was an old man's smile — the smile of a man who had found solace in knowing that no matter how old he got, no matter how weak and world weary he became, he would always remain a few steps ahead of his young friend.

J. D. KING

ODE T A LOST GIRL

where hast thou gone be
boppin beat baby? i
wonder in th bleak winter
of now.

where did you & th spring
of 1961 go? did you follow
th byrds from folk t folk
rock? segue w/allen: beat
generation t flower
chylde? or (alas) did you (sob)
marry a splitlevelgrayflannelad
exec in westchester and raise
2.4?

did you forget (or do
you cherish) th dying
ember of memories: th
3 day amphetamine &
tokay marathon w/ramblin
jack & gregory from your east
5th st pad t coney island t th
bowery (dolphy @ th 5
spot) times sq cabs & sub
ways crisscrossing 5
crazy boros jukebox blasting

mad sex blur days/nights/dawn
crazy talk billy taylor/mulligan?
east 10th st open
ings (a.e. & POP)

le Roi reading/hash & mingus/studying
a wrought iron lamppost frm yr
2nd flr window @ dusk for 1
eternity mingus on the
box still/more hash

where are yr books, thoughts
lps & butterfly
chair? where are
you?

SPARROW, M.F.A.

SOME NOTES ON THE ORIGIN OF "BEAT"

(A transcription of a lecture delivered at The Fez, 10/21/93)

I 've done a lot of research to prepare for this lecture, mostly at the Beat Studies Institute in Worcester, Mass., which is housed in a very modern 16-story building, and surrounded by barbed wire, as it contains many precious documents and artifacts: the ironing board Carolyn Cassady threw at Jack Kerouac on Aug. 19, 1949, in Luma, California; Gregory Corso's baptismal gown, the tractor William Burroughs drove on his farm in Kansas in 1950, the notes to *Dharma Bums*, and the first 14 anuses Allen Ginsberg ever photographed.

At the Beat Studies Institute (which I entered by forging a document claiming I was a post graduate student at Rutgers working on a monograph, "Hipsters in the Air Force") I studied a primary Beat question: the origin of the term "Beat" itself. Kerouac and Ginsberg both claimed the word derived from "beatitude," but it has been documented that they didn't know the word "beatitude" until 1951, 3 years after the term originated. So where did "beat" come from?

Margaret Hosshill suggests it resulted from the competitive nature of the Beat writers. Often Corso, Herbert Huncke, Burroughs and Ginsberg would gather to play bridge, and each would use all his wiles to win. Huncke, particularly, was fond of shouting at Corso: "I beat you, you bastard!" from which the term may have originated.

Ralph Hegglesmith of Clark suggests examining the word "beat" itself, which may be divided into 3 words: "Be a t." The resultant question, of course, is: "What is a 't'?"

A 't,' of course, is a cross. In other words: "Be the cross on which Christ was crucified" — the cross which suffered more than Christ, yet received none of the Glory.

Or it could be read: Be a tee, in other words, a t-shirt. (Remember, this was before t-shirts all had funny sayings on them like: "So much chocolate, so little time.") A t-shirt meant a simple white undergarment — an anti-materialist statement — which, in fact, the Beats often wore, weather permitting, sometimes without pants.

Or: Be a tee, a golf tee, on which the ball rests, and which awaits an uncertain fate. A huge club is poised over it (much like the H-bomb hung over the Beat generation) and the tee may be smashed and uprooted at any minute.

Another possibility is: Be a tea, or, in the hip argot of the time, "Be a marijuana," which is self-explanatory.

My researches led me further to the subject of Neal Cassady. The following paper was originally presented at the Center of Hip and Cool studies in Brattleboro, Vermont.

Neal Cassady: A Reconsideration

Neal Cassady stands at the center of the Beat phenomenon, the way a hole stands at the center of a phonograph record — and similarly, he is invisible.

Beat was purportedly invented by him, and stolen by Jack Kerouac and Allen Ginsberg, yet Neal remains virtually unseen and unheard in *On The Road*. He rarely has a line of dialogue.

Kerouac asks us to take his word about Neal — that he is the greatest fast-speaking, bebop-loving, accelerator-pressing, woman-leaving hipster who ever lived. The miracle is that we *do* take his word. But at some point between high school, when we first encounter *On The Road*, and the age of 40, when we prepare to re-read it, the demon of doubt enters our mind. What if he *wasn't* the greatest fast-speaking, bebop-loving, accelerator-pressing, woman-leaving hipster who ever lived? What if he was just a hick shrouded in a cloak of mystery by 2 New York City intellectuals?

Recently, I began to research this very question. After an exhaustive investigation into Neal's history, I made a startling discovery. Rather than disclose it in a research paper

that will soon be forgotten, I decided to shape it into a song
that may be remembered forever:

wheel,   And   smiled.

This last tonal exercise, originally performed at the Espresso Festival in Buena Vista, California, is an attempt to summarize a 284-page biography of Lew Welch into a 7-line song:

Lew Welch

Lew   Welch   worked   in   advertising,

in   Chicago.   He   wrote   the   phrase

RAID   KILLS   BUGS   DEAD.

Later,   he   moved   to   San   Francisco,

and   became   a   poet,   But   none

of   his   poems   are   as   memorable

As   the   phrase   RAID   KILLS   BUGS   DEAD.

ANN CHARTRES

INTERVIEW WITH ROLLO WHITEHEAD

O n April 1, 1994, Ann Chartres met with Rollo Whitehead at Rollo's Sponge Room on Avenue B across from Tompkins Square Park. Yoko Snapple, Rollo Whitehead's friend and biographer, was there to record the interview as well. It has never before been printed in its entirety.
—The Editors)

AC: Thanks for meeting with me. I guess I'll start with a few background questions. So... who are you and where did you come from?

RW: Well... let's see. My mother was a Dutch-Mexican seamstress who couldn't speak English... but we didn't know *what* the hell she spoke... it was some kinda polyglot thing. She traveled a lot as a kid 'cause my grandfather was friend of Trotsky's so they had to leave Mexico real quick once Stalin got a hold of Trotsky's head! My father was an English country gentleman type of guy... only he was a real mutt... no British in his blood whatsover! He came here from Turkey and his mother, my grandmother... she was Alsace-Lorrainian and Nepalese. When they got here, they couldn't spell his real name... so they asked him to pick a name and he saw some guy reading a book by Alfred North Whitehead... so my grandfather pointed to it and that was the name they gave him. He learned English from being a butler for this English family...the Benways...on the Lower East Side. That's when he started to act like a real proper Victorian type. It was real embarassin' growin' up... 'cause we used to have to drink tea and eat scones and stuff like that...I never got to eat a hot dog or have cotton candy or any of that. And the kids used to pick on me... 'cause of my old man, so I got real tough and macho... kicked my first ass when I was 8. By the time I was 16, I had been to the Tombs so much they started calling me "King Tut."

AC: When did you get involved in writing poetry?

RW: As soon as I could write. My old man got all these books of poetry from guys like Robert Burns and Lord Byron and I hated that shit so I started to write my own...making fun of that style of poetry. When I was about 15...and this is around 1945...I started to get laid all the time. Because of the poetry. See, back then...the guys were all overseas in the war...so kids like me could get lucky once in a while. But I got real lucky 'cause I could impress the girls with poems. I started to cruise the colleges...'cause all the girls used to go there to meet college guys. I looked old for my age so I just told 'em I was a student. They loved it. That's where I met my first two wives.

AC: How did you meet Allen Ginsberg?

RW: I didn't really meet him until after I met Bill Burroughs. Burroughs was really diggin' me...I didn't know it at the time 'cause I never had a fag hit on me before. I was at Columbia one day and he just starts talkin' to me about Rabelais and about Shakespeare and before I know it we're swiggin' beers at a bar nearby. He starts carryin' on about queers and I wonder why. Then his hand goes on my knee and I pop him right in the jaw!

AC: You hit William Burroughs?

RW: Wouldn't be the last time either. They guy couldn't keep his hands to himself when he was on the sauce, y'know? But he learned...eventually.

AC: And Allen Ginsberg?

RW: Well, as I was sayin'...me and Bill used to hang out a lot and swap stories about our families...our friends. He loved my old man 'cause my old man used to tell stories about Dr. Benway, the guy he worked for. Burroughs used to howl all the time...rollin' over in pain with laughter! Those were good times...

Now ya, gotta remember...there were no "poetry cafes" back then...the only poetry readings were going on at high-brow social gatherings and academic sitting rooms and those places. Well, I got this idea to stand out in the middle of the big lawn at Columbia and read my poetry...basically to be a smart-ass, but also 'cause I was piss drunk and feelin' bold. So it's rainin', right? And I wait until the classes break and as soon as the students scurry by, I start blasting my poetry...and I'm makin' up shit, too...I'm ripping everyone a new asshole...democrats, republicans, teachers, police...everyone. I'm goin' on and on...gettin' completely soaked...and a crowd starts to build around me. Some people are laughin' their asses off and others are just mocking me but god-damn that was fun! Well...eventually I just get so wild that I start walking towards the street and there's about 50 people followin' me and we got this train walkin' out into the streets...fuckin' incredible. I wish I had a picture of that day. Man...

Anyway...the cops broke it up and they almost took me in for drunk and disorderly. But this kid steps in and starts telling them that I'm really an assistant teacher at Columbia and this was actually a field trip and all this bullshit. And it turns out it was Allen. This meek little Jewish kid was all fired up sayin', "Man, that was great! You're amazing!" Meanwhile, this kid can't cross the street without holding your hand! No balls whatsover. And he buys me lunch, gets me even more drunk and introduces me to some of his other friends...Like Lucien, and Jack and some others. Well... before I go home that night...drunk off my ass...I give Allen all the poems I brought with me. I didn't give a shit about 'em. And I never thought twice about them until I started seein' altered versions of them appearing in books years later! But that's another story...

AC: Rollo, you've often been called the "greatest unknown Beat." Why is this so?

RW: Hmmm...that's an interesting question, coming from you, Ann. I mean, you of all people know why. After all, *you're* the one who seems to leave me out of every essay on Beat writing, every book on Beat literature, and every friggin' retrospective!!!

AC: Yes, but I was only following orders!

RW: And you're not the only one, either...there's you, Grauerholz, Mailer did it too, all those friggin' "Beat Journey" things with Arthur and Kit. And where the hell am I in all this? Nowhere...but that's okay. Why'd you bother lookin' for me now anyway? I know why...'cause you're nervous that the Unbearables are gonna be the skunks at your little garden party. Well...let me tell you...you and the rest of your sycophantic kind will be nothing more than fucking poetry housewives once this "Beat fucking revival" is over. Oh... damn...I gotta fart...

AC: You really don't have to be so hostile, Rollo...I'm only trying to get to the bottom of this. Don't act so high and mighty...you aren't exactly Mr. Ethics either. I mean, Allen and Gregory both told me about all your violent outbursts, all your debaucheries...your attitude...you are a really lecherous and barbaric old man, do you know that? Like what you did to the original manuscript-roll for *On the Road*...

RW: Oh, that...so? I had to wipe my ass...I had the runs that day and Allen's got this thing sitting in his bathroom

so I go and use it like I had to. And anyway, that book is shit
...the worst thing Jack wrote and he knew it. One time he
told me that he wrote it because Allen said it would get him
very popular with college kids. But we know Allen was talking about college BOYS, not girls. Hey...did you know that
me and Jack, when he was writing *On the Road* used to make
prank calls to Burroughs to pass the time? That was a friggin' scream, I tell ya! I knew what Jack was doin', so don't go
and give me this stupid whining shit about what I did to that
roll of paper...cause you don't know the scoop...

AC: Oh, really. And what about your claims that you
wrote Allen's poems...like "Howl"?

RW: I did! But I hated it so much that I chucked it in the
friggin' trash! And Allen picks it up and he goes, "Hey, could
I use this for scrap paper?" and I said, sure! And then he
went to San Francisco...

AC: How can you prove this?

RW: How can you prove *Allen* wrote it?

AC: His name and handwriting are on the first draft...
you can see where he made his corrections...he...

RW: Gimme that piece of paper over there. [Takes paper
and begins to write on it.] What does it say on this piece of
paper?

AC: *"Howl" by Allen Ginsberg.* So?

RW: What's the difference between the so-called "first
draft" and this? If you weren't there to see him write it, how
do you know he did?

AC: This is ridiculous, his handwriting and signature are
valid...

RW: So? A good forger could forge a Rembrandt!

AC: Well, I for one don't believe you wrote "Howl."

RW: Okay, Fine with me.

AC: I can't do this...you are an absurd old man.

RW: And you're a sexless housefrau with a degree...

(At this point, Ann Chartres jumps out of her chair, snatches her tape recorder from the table, and leaves Rollo's Sponge Room in a huff. To this day, she refuses to have anything to do with the Unbearables. She also vehemently denies ever having conducted the above interview.)

MICHAEL CALLAHAN

"REBEL VOICES SPEAK AGAIN"
A GATHERING OF THE BEATS

WASHINGTON DC — National Portrait Gallery, April 27, 1996

I wanted to bring the beer. Frank told me I should hold off. There would be beer at the reception, and it wouldn't be a good idea to carry any bottles into the reading. Security might give me a hard time, even if I had a press pass. I left the beer behind. I decided it wouldn't be in our best interest to upset any rebels.

We were greeted at the door by a slender gray haired woman with thick glasses and a watery handshake. "Here," she smiled, handing us our passes along with a handful of flyers and photographs. She turned to Frank with a thoughtful description of each black and white glossy as she produced them. "Oh. This one is called *Last Gathering of the Beats*. It's so wonderful! Look at Corso there, and the look in Kerouac's face... and here's one of Allen sitting on a sofa, it was taken in New York—"

"Who's the guy on his lap?" I asked.

She raised her skinny eyebrows and glanced at me above the rim of her glasses with a solid oh-quit-pulling-my-leg-you-know-better-than-that look. My guess is that she simply didn't know.

"OK. The reading's already started. You might have a hard time getting in, and, of course, you'll have to be very quiet. Just head back down this hall, take the first stairway on your right..."

We nodded and made our way upstairs. We had no trouble at all getting in, press passes or no. The security guards were much more interested in protecting the antique paintings lining the hall; poets, apparently, meant nothing to them.

The poets were reading in a large theater on a high platform — not quite a stage — flanked by the most elaborate frieze I have ever seen, gilded with gold before a line of carefully pleated evergreen velvet drapery. *Well,* I couldn't help but think, *these rebels have sure come a long way.*

I was silently relieved that we arrived late at the reading. I was more relieved that the poets were reading no more than three or four poems apiece. There were eight poets (not including David Amram) and ten references to Kerouac (not including David Amram). I half-expected these guys to surprise us with a Ouija board as a 'surprise guest reader.' Maybe later there would be a seance. The way these rebels spoke, it certainly seemed possible.

There was something bleakly fascinating about a roomful of hippie college freshmen and Birkenstock-wearing cafe regulars all sitting in the Smithsonian National Portrait Gallery listening raptly to eight old men read old poetry that was either impossible to understand or painfully meaningless. *Are they being enriched?* I wondered. *Entertained?* It was a mystery I didn't quite care enough about to solve.

I was, however, impressed by how thoughtful I became after listening to beat poetry for about fifteen minutes. My mind was desperately reaching for the relief of any external stimulus aside from the numbing drone of unintelligible wordplay. I imagine an isolation tank would have a similar effect (hopefully without any poetry). I was hungry for words with meaning, images I could access. Although nobody else would ever admit it, I believe the rest of the audience all shared in this cruel sensory deprivation. This is part of the reason why the crowd would burst into enthusiastic scattered laughter every time a lowbrow literary reference was made:

Whenever I need just a quickie
I open and read some of Dickie...

Oh, that's rich. Stop, stop. You're killing me. Of course, another reason to laugh at radically humorless tripe like that is that by laughing you acknowledge you *understand* the reference, which all but indirectly proclaims your intellectual prowess and admirable literacy. This is in and of itself a barrel of monkeys. Or so I came to realize.

To be entirely fair, there were two readers who made intelligent sense, and seemed appropriately out of place: Kenneth Koch and Lawrence Ferlinghetti. Kenneth read concise verse about baseball, and Lawrence shared some very well thought out sketches. Neither of them made reference to Kerouac.

Closing the show, David Amram appeared with some uncomfortable looking jazz musicians and impressed the lot of us by extolling the virtues of Benjamin Franklin and masturbatory improvisation (?). All this, and he can play four different instruments...sometimes at the same time. He reminded me of one of those Looney Tunes one-man-band outfits; hands on an accordion, crash cymbals between the knees, bass drum strapped to his back. Right on, Daffy.

There was no beer at the reception, but there was wine. I immediately filled myself a glass and just as immediately stumbled unwittingly into a conversation with a fat, proud drunkard who kept showing me that his cane secretly concealed a razor-sharp sword. This wore thin after about thirty seconds, and I hastily excused myself under the pretext of wanting to see some masterfully constructed paper silhouettes.

I caught up with Frank and we were soon approached by Mr. Goodwill himself, David Amram. "So...are you guys going back to New York tonight?" he asked casually, all smiles. If he needed a ride that badly, he should have just come right out and asked for one.

Frank took out the photographs he received earlier and started thumbing through them. A sharp looking man with a cute oriental woman by his side stepped over. "Hey, can I see those?" he asked.

"Sure," answered Frank, handing them over.

The man rotated them in his hands. "Well, I'll be damned..." he trailed off.

"Are you in any of those?" I asked.

"In them? No. I took the damn things. I'm a photographer." He handed them back to Frank. "They didn't even give me credit. Son of a bitch."

Rebels.

Later in the evening, as the starry eyed deadheads slowly begin to filter out, I got into an interesting conversation with publisher Ron Whitehead about The Unbearables — a group of anti-beat New York poets.

"Do you know about those guys?" I asked, figuring this was a pretty small community.

"Oh yeah, yeah, I do." He nodded knowingly. He told me that one of them (The Unbearables) wrote a story a few years back about a fictional character named Rollo Whitehead who was a poorly veiled underhanded mockery of the beat writers. Allen Ginsberg somehow got ahold of this questionable fiction, and made the immediate assumption that Ron Whitehead was responsible for its creation. This created strong tensions between the two of them until Ron could effectively convince Allen that he had nothing to do with it. "The funny thing is," concluded Ron, "that I never met the guy who wrote that damn thing."

"Are you angry about it"?"

"No, not really."

"Well, let me get your mailing address. I'll get you in touch with the author."

"Sure, sure. Hey. I don't have a pen."

"Hold on."

I turned to whoever was standing next to me, who, coincidentally, turned out to be Allen Ginsberg. "Hey," I said, "have you got a pen?"

Allen's beady eyes lit up. "I don't feel like signing anymore autographs," he hastily replied.

"No," I said, "I asked you for a *pen*."

INVOICE

MAKE CHECK PAYABLE TO:

Allen Ginsberg
P. O. Box 528
Stuyvesant Station
New York, NY 10009

SOLD TO				SHIPPED TO		
Stanford University Libraries				Special Collections/Green Library		
STREET & NO.				STREET & NO.		
Green Library, Room 351				Stanford University		
CITY	STATE		ZIP	CITY	STATE	ZIP
Stanford, CA 94305-6004				Stanford, CA 94305-6004		

CUSTOMER'S ORDER	SOLD BY	TERMS		F.O.B.	DATE	
	A. G.	pay on receipt			9-7-94	

1 collection of personal papers, including 4513 letters, 8751 manuscripts, 507 drawings, 3678 photographs, 703 books, 1 pair of
worn-out sneakers, 2 pairs of torn blue jeans, 1 T-shirt briefly
worn by Jack Kerouac (never washed), 3 pairs of Gregory Corso's
underwear, 14 broken Indian musical instruments, 2 arms, 2 eyes,
2 lips, 2 balls, 1 penis, 1 spleen, 1 colon, 1 anus, 1,481,814
business cards, and other remains.

TOTAL: $1,000,000.00

REDIFORM
7L721

MIKE GOLDEN

THE UNBEAR-
ABLE BEATNIKS
OF LIGHT
GET REAL!

In this day and age certain truths are not always self evident, but the *Unbearable* beatniks of light are on a roll
tonight. Truth is in sight, because tonight on the occasion of their return to New York City, on the occasion of
their first meeting in over two years, they've unanimously
agreed to give up the old ways, the old thoughts, the old
attachments that held them prisoners for so long to a time
and place that never really existed as anything other than a
state of mind, despite media hype and career conspiracies to
the contrary. We're talking about *downtown*, hipsters, as if
you couldn't have guessed.

The *Unbearables* have been on the road for the last couple of years, choosing the apex of the scene to split for different parts unknown, unglued and yes, most of all,
unhyped, hipsters. Like dust to the wind they got gone just
before the bottom fell out of the East Village gallery and performance scene, riding their memories of hot times in the
old Alphabet Town off into the existential sunset, leaving the
Club scene floggers behind to celebrate for nothing more
than the-glory-of-the-glory.

Yo! In the old-old *good-old-days* (remember *those were the
days, my friends, the days we thought would never end...*),
the *Unbearables*, who are not really beatniks, but a free-
floating, in-your-face Temporary Autonomous Zone of Black
Humorists, Immediatists, Neoists and Beer Mystics, used to
meet every other Tuesday night in certain downtown water-
ing holes and drown themselves in nostalgia for, what else,
but *the-good-old-days*. Certainly a disease of the spirit, hipsters, which on reflection, everyone now agrees, comes out
sounding like a cross between Dodge City Saturday Night
and an unenforceable DMZ right in the heart of Junkieland.
Ah, but we're starting to toss grenades before we even choose
up sides...

First, their name—*The Unbearable Beatniks of Light*,
which came to the original foursome courtesy of a spooner-
ism one sloshed night in the old Tin Pan Alley, while noting
that for some unfathomable reason all the really groovy
chicks were into Kundera's *The Unbearable Lightness of
Being*. As individuals or a group, they were always caught

somewhere in the middle—too young to be real beatniks, too old to be hippies, too late to be punks, but always hanging out on one cutting edge or another all their lives. They first started hanging with each other two years before it became obvious the end of the last new wave was the next old hat. And then realized nothing else could even be tried-on, much less embraced, until the corpse was buried. In previous incarnations they were all seemingly involved in what can now be generically classified as the downtown scene. Since the *unbearable* gaffe first occurred, and since at heart they are all democratic anarchists, they pick their beatnik code names (Jack, Neal, Allen, Bill, Gregory, Herbert, etc.) out of a hat every meeting, so last time if you were Jack this time you might be Neal or Allen or Bill, or Gregory, etc.

"What this does," tonight's Allen explains to me, "is it takes us out of ourselves, out of indulging in our own personal problems." Tonight's Allen has just spent the last two years living in suburbia, saving his marriage by helping his wife's brother open a shopping center outside of Youngstown, Ohio. "You know what I'm talking about," he says. *"The wife flipped it, I didn't get the raise, the lease ran out and the scumbags are raising the rent from 289.50 to 14-hundred.* At the same time, by changing names every week, none of us gets trapped in any one persona."

"This way," tonight's Neal explains, "it stays sort of a healthy schizoid exercise as opposed to a real schizoid existence." Tonight's Neal, who used to be a well known SoHo bartender before he moved to Barcelona, originally came to the Lower East Side from England in '75, virtually penniless. He likes to remember little tidbits like when the subway and slice of pizza both cost 35 cents. "I thought it was the bloody law they had to cost the same thing!" he laughs.

Tonight's Allen, who used to manage a bookstore in what he calls "the heart of the beast," remembers fondly, "almost too fondly," the days when the Lower East Side was considered "no man's land. The Hell's Angels ran the neighborhood. Junkies and shooting parlours proliferated."

"And that doesn't even go back to the days of The Electric Circus." Tonight's Jack comes back to the table after he's finished reading from his novel in the back room. A well known DJ before he packed it in to move to Paris to write "The Great American Novel," he first came to the Lower East Side 21 years ago, from East Jesus, Nebraska, to freak out! But it was too late. The Fillmore was closed. The heads had all splattered then scattered, got gone back to the land and left the streets to the speed freaks.

"It's been a while since I've heard that word," muses tonight's Bill, a tall, elegant, anthropology professor who spends most of his time out of the city studying shamanism in remote corners of the world.

"What word?" tonight's Jack asks. "Freak?"

"No, speed." Tonight's Bill smiles. "Remember speed?"

"The real thing," tonight's Neal smiles. "I haven't heard the word in 10 years. What happened to speed? It just sort of disappeared."

"Cocaine," tonight's Allen wheezes. "The non-addictive yuppie elixir. Thank God I'm allergic to it."

Suddenly a loud roar comes from the crowd as tonight's Gregory comes out of the back room and climbs up on top of the bar, to read an old favorite to the hungry mob.

"Not again!" Tonight's Bill puts his hands over his eyes. "He's not going to do his—"

"HIGH! HIGH!" tonight's Gregory roars from the top of his tonsils. "HOW HIGH CAN YOU FLY BEFORE YOU DIE?" he sings out, then pounds his chest like he's Tarzan and has just spotted The Bitch Goddess Muse on the other side of the river. He lets loose a loud soul cleansing call to all the animas of the East and West Villages, then does a perfect swan dive off the bar, splattering head first on the concrete!

The *Unbearables* at the table turn back away from the human puddle on the floor, and one by one, lift their hands like diving judges—an eight from tonight's Neal, a nine from tonight's Allen, a six from tonight's Bill, a seven from tonight's Jack—and then get back to business as usual.

By the time tonight's Gregory has been scraped off the floor, loaded on a slab and carted away, everyone's reliving a different way to find their own separate reality, though it should be pointed out to all *you* undercover DEA agents out there, the *Unbearables* are drug free now, considering their tastes, bouts, marriages and indulgences with pharmaceuticals & herbs as merely phases, rights of passage they had to undergo to get to the condition their condition is in now.

"We're just pawns in the detoxification of America," tonight's Bill insists. "These memories of the way things are are as bad as any addiction I've ever had."

"Worse than tobacco," tonight's Jack wheezes.

"Maudlin, sentimental, and politically incorrect," tonight's Allen moans.

"Which is exactly why I miss them!" tonight's Neal proclaims. "I like doing things for the bloody toss of it! That's why I moved here in the first place. Where's your bloody spirit, mates? Have we turned into a coven of wussies? Isn't there one bloody gesture among us?"

"Listen to Neal, he's got a wild hair tonight!" Tonight's Jack laughs. "But hey, there ain't no more America to bang-bang, much less a Neuvo York. Not that Paris is that much better now, but at least it looks good. And hey, nobody can say the Frogs don't give good 'tude. In reality they may be vapid, they may be shallow, they may be total blanks, but you've got to admit their shells are cool. Here everything and everyone is redundant. Nothing but the same ghouls and necrophiles on the club scene, takin' care of their egos, baby. Takin' care of their egos."

"A bit harsh, old boy. Some of my best friends are ghouls and necrophiles," tonight's Neal grimaces. "Matter of fact, I do believe it's my heritage as well."

The addiction kicks back in then. The good old days, before they realize it, are back. The glory of Darinka, The Shuttel, 8 BC, all sacrifices to gentrification, become a litany; Normandy, Anzio, just a regular *Guadalcanal Diary*, hipsters.

Before long the *Unbearables* are sloshing through the mindfields of memory: The Feast of Unbraining at The Theatre for the New City, Don Cherry blowing The Shuttel's lights out all night long, Karen Finley's first yam, Seymour Krim *Making It* for the last time at Darinka, the performances and readings and parties in the Rivington School's sculpture garden, the New Year's Day marathon at The Poetry Project, when tonight's *Gregory* was standing in a long line to get a urinal when the *real* Gregory himself stumbles in, takes one look at the line, then swaggers straight over to the sink, unzips and lets fly as he goes into a 10 minute riff that freezes everyone's dorks in their fists, on why most guys find it impossible to piss when somebody's talking to them... And of course, *what's his name's* birthday party at The Palladium. "That was the beginning of the end," tonight's Allen ruefully sighs. "*The Eye* was flying high—"

"Oh mi-oh-mi!" tonight's Jack sings.

"Literary night in the Mike Todd Room."

"MC'd by The King of the Yuppies."

"Bright Lights, Big Nostrils."

"That pissed a lot of people off."

"It's one thing to gentrify the bloody landscape, but the bloody art should be sacred!"

"You're just jealous."

"Good first line."

"You're just jealous. It's not malicious," tonight's Jack mocks. "You've been invited to a party. Naturally there's a reading. You're not asked to participate. But there's an open bar and free food. You're immediately attracted to the suckling pigs. Just then the star comes on. You feel sorry for him. You feel envious of him. You feel sorry for him again. The crowd surges up against the stage. Drooling, flipping spit off the tips of their fingers at his head: He's an easy target. Like any icon, his head is huge. Almost as big as Richard Burton's was, and he hasn't even learned to move it yet. Just stands there and takes it, proudly pissed. Ready to *Mailer* the whole mob at once."

"So you want to be the bloody *Man*, do you?"

"You hyperventilate. Remember the curse of talent. Only the good die young. What if you were Rimbaud in a past life? Do you remember what fame was like? Or how the cliché tasted on your tongue?"

"Sweet and sour pork. Twins. Mirrors of rejection. You're looking at yourself looking at yourself looking at yourself;

not a pretty picture, but *They* might buy it all the same. *If your conceit is as good as his.*"

"You lift the pig off the table."

"Would you like to dance, my dear?"

"Would you like to dance, my dear?" There's an echo in the room.

The *Unbearables* are cooking now. Jamming on their own addiction.

"You've already been famous for five minutes, now what, asshole?"

"Get a lime juice commercial!"

"Make a movie."

"Open a gallery."

"Start a band."

As if on cue, they start singing: *"Pull my daisy, tip my cup, all my doors are open... Cut my thoughts for coconuts, all my eggs are broken..."*

I seem to have missed something in the translation. The dancing pig. Did tonight's Jack did, or did tonight's Jack didn't throw the pig?

"No way, man! I was just getting inside the story. Getting inside the cat's head who threw it. That's how things get twisted!"

"It was bloody unbelievable," tonight's Neal laughs. *"Bright Lights* wasn't even on stage when it happened. Some little guy reading something nobody's listening to. Just getting it on, and getting it over as fast as he can, when all of a sudden this pig's head—there was nothing left but the head—comes flying through the air, right in front of his bloody eyes."

"Stage left!"

The signal to split, on more than one level. It's time for the *Unbearables* to find that next whiskey bar. But not before making a vow, deciding to make one final gesture, as an ode to their glorious past.

Dressed head to toe in traditional hipster black, they trudge angst ridden through the light mist, as they debate what action to take as they bop east across Houston. *What can they do? What one tiny gesture can they make to release themselves from the past, at the same time they honor it?*

Perhaps liberate *The New Yorker's* po-et-ry from medi-oc-rity? Though that idea they concede is almost as mediocre as the poetry they would like to liberate. Perhaps put the beatniks, the real beatniks on trial? Turn *The Crimes of the Beats* into the Nuremberg of Bohemia: Call out Burroughs for copping W. C. Fields act, and Ginsberg for being the original Maynard G. Krebs in the gray flannel beret—always hyping, hyping, hyping the myth, then selling, selling, selling it as the only viable alternative to the polluted mainstream, and of course Jackie boy himself for claiming he wrote *On The Road* in one sitting; a lie that ruined three whole generations of novelists gobbling speed to duplicate the feat of the beat that never really went down in anything short of seven drafts, maybe... Or perhaps each one of the *Unbearables* themselves selling out by getting their own personal sponsors? Writing letters to Pepsi Cola, IBM, General Motors, Conde Naste, all over corporate America, and asking their worst ideological enemies for funding to fight the rise of corporate America. Then hold an annual Telethon on Cable, and call it *The Night of a Thousand Sponsors.*

But all these ideas are obviously down the road, not on it. For the moment, the now, on the next beat they decide, unanimously decide, to liberate St. Marks Place. From *what,* they're not sure. But it must be done, there's no doubt about that! Though the *how* of making a Revolutionary act in America in the 1990s is not that easy. Not that easy at all. Back in the late 60s the Yippies changed the name of the street from St. Marks to St. Marx, but the Marxists are free now, the *Commies* all want to be *Cappies,* so that *McGuffin* won't work anymore. It's as dead and gone as that defunct breed once known as "hip capitalists."

Swaying back and forth now, they stand on the corner of St. Marks and Second Avenue, in front of Gem Spa, invoking the ghost of poet Ted Berrigan simultaneously gobbling speed and sucking up an egg cream, as they stare incredulously across the street at something that looks like it was beamed down from a shopping mall in Paramus.

"That's it!" tonight's Jack snaps.

"Close The bloody Gap!" tonight's Neal roars.

"No more pastels!" tonight's Allen wails.

"Send them back to the burbs!" tonight's Bill bops.

"Blow them to smithereens!" tonight's Neal cackles.

"You mean actually bomb them?" tonight's Jack asks.

"Have you got a better idea?" tonight's Bill snarls.

"We could pool our money, and put a Banana Republic in across the street, to drive them out of business."

Tonight's beatnik turns to me and says, "Don't quote me on that."

The *Unbearables* look down at the sidewalk, down at the concrete. Then in mass, slowly, very slowly trudge west, back in the direction they came from.

In the middle of the block, they duck inside The Grassroots, for one last round.

Tonight's Allen turns to tonight's Jack and sighs, before they push through the doors: "Obviously, things aren't the same anymore."

Tonight's Jack laughs: "If they ever were."

"If they ever were," tonight's Bill echoes.

"If they ever were..."

ALFRED VITALE

THE MOVEMENT THAT ALMOST WAS: UNBEARABLE INFLUENCES ON BEAT LITERATURE

(The full version of this paper was originally presented at The International Symposium on 20th Century Bohemianism held earlier this year in Sarajevo. Due to a mortar shell blast, the Symposium was cut short as most of the participants were blown to pieces. Alfred Vitale narrowly escaped by hiding behind Wolf Blitzer. This is a condensed version of the original.)

O ften literary movements appear simultaneously and compete with each other in trying to appeal to the masses. During the early 1950s, such a situation did indeed occur. However, only one of these emerged as an accepted movement. In this essay, I will illustrate some examples of this emergence while it was still forming... a time when the two movements were related and, in fact, practically dependent on each other. The two movements were the "Beats" (Kerouac, Burroughs, Ginsberg, Corso, Cassady, Holmes, DiPrima, Rexroth, Whitehead and the TV character Maynard G. Krebs, et al.) and the "Unbearables" (Kolm, Feast, Rapaport, Golden, plantenga, Wierzbicki, Sirowitz, Mesmer, Watson, Litzky, Sparrow, et. al.)

A brief introduction to either of these two groups is unnecessary since there is plenty of available literature on both of them (although works dealing with the Unbearables are difficult to find since they appear mostly in small press, underground magazines, and on bathroom walls) and it would be redundant here. What I will focus on is not how these groups were unique, but rather how they were *related* ...and more importantly, how they interacted both on a personal level and on the level of literature.

An interesting little story may help shed some light on the type of relationship the two groups had. Some time in the early 1950s, Jack Kerouac was in the bathroom at a diner in New York's Hell's Kitchen. On his way out, he bumped into Mike Golden. Golden had known Kerouac from the days when Golden was a shoe salesman in Kerouac's hometown of Lowell. Norman Mailer, in his essay "The Black Honkey," writes of that meeting:

Golden had sold Kerouac the shoes that Kerouac took "on the road" a while later. Golden shakes Kerouac's hand and says, "How's things with you guys?" (meaning the Columbia crowd of Kerouac, Ginsberg, Burroughs, et al.) and Kerouac says, "Oh...we're all doin' pretty much the same...no shit goin' down here that's not like shit goin' down anywhere else, I figure..." and Golden says, "Man...you guys are just UNBEARABLE!...Maybe you should call yourselves that!"

Kerouac thinks for a minute...in his mind he's saying, "Hmmm...Unbearable. Let's see...it's a little long and hard to spell...how marketable is it? Unbearablenik? Nahhhh...it'll never work." He says out loud. "No...you guys should call YERSELVES that!" and the two go off on their merry ways.

Ten minutes later, at the same coffee shop, Kerouac is over heard telling someone, "Man...I'm so beat!" And the rest is history, as they say.

A footnote to that story. Golden had written a book called *On the Highway* about his travels with Jim Feast across the USA. But, on its way to the publisher, the manuscript was lost in the mail.

Kerouac, a year later, will write *On The Road*.

Early on, as Burroughs was holing up near Columbia and being visited by the budding Kerouac and Ginsberg, there were often late night intellectual soirees with Rollo Whitehead, Peter Lamborn Wilson and Jose Padua. Whitehead would later say that Burroughs was extremely attracted to him (Whitehead) but Rollo was not interested... Burroughs, now scorned by the object of his desires, turns to Ginsberg for romantic relations...and in a letter from Burroughs to Whitehead (1952) he writes

...party in the first part wishes party inna second part to reciprocate the malodorous advances of my queer aversions... what say you?...if you feel that romantic involvement would be a mistake (a strictly Freudian denial of things, I would say ...perhaps some Reichian therapy would help. I can make suggestions.) then I shall be forced into baboon-like behavior (it is a fact that the male baboon will, while trying to snare the rutting female of the species, attempt to mate with an undesirable female in an attempt to stir a simian sense of jealously in intended target) ...cut to east St. Louis bar full of inadequate purple-assed baboons on roccoco bar stools...one say to other, "wouldn'tya know the old gash had the aftosa!" "aftosa? hell, boy, that a cow's disease!" "it is? no wonder she reject my advance!"...what i mean, Rollo, is that I have Allen standing by in the wings waiting for the day I make him and it may be a comin' soon...yessirree...target A rejecting me, so I resort to lesser mate. oh well, son cosas de la vida!...

Burroughs had many encounters with the Unbearables. A memorable one occurred when Burroughs had called up Ron Kolm to see if Kolm could get Burroughs a feature in *Appearances* magazine. While he was on the phone, one of Ron's children had taken the cat and stuck it in the oven. Meanwhile, Ron's other child was gnawing on Ron's shins... Burroughs commented, "Ron, you gotta keep those kids outta there...it sounds like a rumpus room." Obviously, this is the basis for the Ron's Rumpus Room routine in *Naked Lunch.*

...danny the redhead gets up on the platform and throws wooden blocks covered with mayan codices at the spectators in their squat wooden chairs. his brother, the notorious lego trafficker, takes a crayon outta Lucy Bradshinkel's headpiece and doodles in etruscan across the monocoled forehead of A.J. Kittens are tossed about helter skelter as the boys run amok in the nursery school.

"Keep at 'em boys," says a smiling Benway, "just a few more lacerations and that kitty cat will be as good as a South East Asian buffet!"

Ron fell out of favor with Burroughs because of a story he had gotten published in an obscure literary journal called *Rant*. The story was called "The Man in the William Tell Hat"... a poke at Burroughs' shooting of his wife. Many people found this story amusing, although Burroughs wasn't one of them.

Ginsberg comes back into the picture with his legendary first performance of "Howl" in San Francisco. According to Ginsberg, the poem was originally written for Hal Sirowitz and was really called "Hal"... but in all the noise during that reading, the title was misconstrued as "Howl" and the name stuck. In fact the first line indicates a Sirowitzian influence:

I saw the best minds of my generation destroyed by madness, Mother said ...

Ginsberg and Sirowitz were tight for a long time... and it's a little known fact that Ginsberg stayed with Sirowitz for a few months back in the late 50s... under the condition that he tell Sirowitz's mother that he was a traveling Rabbi (Sirowitz's mother was staunchly anti-poetry and never knew of her son's "alternative lifestyle"). Hal wrote a poem, in later years, about those months with Ginsberg in his house.

Don't disturb the Rabbi while he's sleeping, Mother said, or he might get mad and
tell God to curse you with blindness.

And then you couldn't see the words of
the Torah and you'd have to convert to
Catholicism since Catholics don't need
to see because they can stroke the statues
and know which ones they are praying to.
You can't do that with the Torah.
But you'd have to go to Bingo on Friday nights
with your seeing-eye-dog.
I think you would get a lot of sympathy
and maybe even a wife.

Sirowitz first met Jack Kerouac in 1954. He and Tsaurah Litzky flew out to San Francisco to take part in the first National Poetry Slam, hosted by Bob Holman. There were only three poets and no audience. Holman posed the famous question, "If poets slam and nobody hears it, is it still a slam?" Hal and Tsaurah had made arrangements to stay with Kerouac for the week. But Kerouac, in his usual drunken stupor, didn't realize what day it was and so the surprised Kerouac stood there, naked, as Hal and Tsaurah waltzed into the apartment. Tsaurah tells us:

So we walk in and Jack's standing there in the buff and I look him over and I go, "Jeez…Jack, you could've at least taken me to dinner first!"

For the next week, while Tsaurah cavorted with Kerouac, Hal tried to convince a young Diane DiPrima that if they had sex, he *wouldn't* write a poem about it. She declined, but he wrote a poem about it anyway.

Hal had found a friend, though, in Kerouac. Kerouac was very much taken with Hal's sense of humor and deadpan attitude. In fact, before he tried Buddhism, Kerouac even toyed with Judaism under the tutelage of Sirowitz. But Hal's influence eventually became a burden to Kerouac, who was busy writing another book. Sirowitz suggested a title, but Kerouac didn't like the sound of *Shiksa Bums*, so he changed religions, changed the title and stuck with it. From then on, he developed an anti-Semitic attitude and resented Sirowitz. Anne Waldman told how at Naropa, Kerouac would even attack Ginsberg's Jewish background with verbal abuse and insulting poetry. A typical example of this anti-Semitic ridicule was found in one of Kerouac's notebooks. This is an excerpt of, as he mockingly titled it, "The 239th and 240th Torahs of the Jerusalem City Blues":

Hal Sirowitz
looked
like Moses
in his boy scout fatigues
and stone tablets...

Kerouac also poked fun at Ron Kolm. This was actually because Ron had to break the news to Kerouac that one of his poems wasn't getting into the next issue of Michael Carter's magazine *RedTape*. Kerouac was a little sore since Carter had promised to publish the piece. The only reason he didn't publish the piece was because he was completely zonked on Nemby's when he said it. But, nonetheless, Kolm felt the brunt. Kerouac writes in his notebook:

THE ESSENTIALS OF SPONTANEOUS KOLM
1...that's good, that's good, that's good, that's good
2...yeah, i hear ya, yeah, i hear ya, i hear ya, i hear ya
3...can ya flip me a copy, can ya flip me a copy, can ya flip me a copy
4...no, you're in, that's no problem, that's no problem, that's no problem
5...lemme shut up, lemme shut up, lemme shut up, lemme shut up

bart plantenga was an Unbearable with a late-night TV show that featured odd acts such as, in later years, William Shatner singing "Lucy in the Sky with Diamonds," as well as Blowfly (interestingly enough, there were so many "bleeps" in that episode that it sounded like one, big long "bleep" and people mistook it for a notice of the Emergency Broadcast System). He was the first person to interview the Beats on television (years before Steve Allen). But rather than flood the program with BeBop Jazz, he choose to play British Skiffle

Music, which didn't sit well with Beat Poetry. Kerouac, disgusted by his performance of "The Wheel of the Quivering Meat Conception" read to a background of "Oh, The Party's On In South End, Chap!" stormed off the set in the middle of the show. plantenga, the quick-witted opportunist, brought out three Unbearables dressed as belly dancers. One was Bonny Finberg, another was Carol Wierzbicki. They enjoyed their first TV appearance and whooped it up for the studio audience. But the third dancer was Carl Watson...and Watson was not so thrilled. In fact, rumor has it that he was so embarrassed by his performance that he moved to the outskirts of Sheboygan the very next day.

Rollo Whitehead stands out as one of the few people who managed to peacefully coexist with both groups. Whitehead was so versatile and well-liked, that when Ferlinghetti offered to publish a City Lights Pocket Poet book of Whitehead's works, Rollo declined in order to stay in the Unbearables' good graces, stating:

I am not a beat. I am not unbearable. I am just Unbearably Beat.

Unfortunately Mr. Whitehead has left the public eye and lives in seclusion along with Yoko Snapple, one of his closest friends and co-author of *Don't Bother Me, Brother: The Memoirs of Rollo Whitehead*, which features an introduction in Iambic Dodecameter by Sparrow.

There were other memorable Beat/Unbearable relationships...immortalized in pages of poems, stories, essays and books. Perhaps in time, Viking will publish *The Unbearable Reader* and instead of goatees and berets, fashion trends will emulate the Unbearables' lack-of-fashion sense, and college kids with rebellious attitudes will be carrying around copies of *Confessions of a Beer Mystic*, *Welcome to the Barbecue*, *Flipped Kiss*, *The Occupations*, *T.A.Z.*, *Mother Said*, *One Size Fits All*, *Ego Monkey*, *Skirted Issues*, *Red Blade*, *RANT*, and *Pink Pages*, instead of trying to impress with the easily accessible Rimbaud, Bukowski, Kerouac, or Burroughs.

Rollo Whitehead

Brilliant, swerving flecks of steam
hissing low like satyrs
come and smally
lift and silky
blow a hambone.

Blow a table, carve and
shards and silver
knife, spoon, fork
and drum.
Metalflake. Dreams of

Pistons lifting
silver. Dreams of
metalflake.